God Honoring Finances

God Honoring Finances

✦

What The Bible Tells You About Managing your Money

Philip S. Wilson

iUniverse, Inc.
New York Lincoln Shanghai

God Honoring Finances
What The Bible Tells You About Managing your Money

Copyright © 2007 by Philip S. Wilson

iUniverse books may be ordered through booksellers or by contacting:

iUniverse
2021 Pine Lake Road, Suite 100
Lincoln, NE 68512
www.iuniverse.com
1-800-Authors (1-800-288-4677)

The information, ideas, and suggestions in this book are not intended to render professional advice. Before following any suggestions contained in this book, you should consult your personal accountant or other financial advisor. Neither the author nor the publisher shall be liable or responsible for any loss or damage allegedly arising as a consequence of your use or application of any information or suggestions in this book.

ISBN-13: 978-0-595-42181-7 (pbk)
ISBN-13: 978-0-595-86519-2 (ebk)
ISBN-10: 0-595-42181-4 (pbk)
ISBN-10: 0-595-86519-4 (ebk)

Printed in the United States of America

Contents

1

The Need for Good Advice

Glance at the newspaper headlines. Companies are less committed to employees. Employees are less committed to employers. Job security is nonexistent. The days of retiring with the initial company that hired you for your first job are over.

Costs of employee benefits are shifting to the shoulders of workers. To have a comfortable retirement, you must save money yourself. No longer can you depend on a company retirement pension. Companies have little incentive to provide long-term benefits because workers do not stay with one employer for very long. Workers tend to jump around. To have adequate health insurance, most workers must share the costs with their employers.

We want it now. Personal debt and bankruptcies are at record highs. The purchase of goods with credit cards creates a pattern of overspending. The constant desire for more of everything has put an end to most personal savings. Furthermore, people do not pay off their credit cards anymore. Many people find sport in locating teaser rates for their credit cards.

Look at the example set by the government: politicians frequently are overspending, creating deficits that our children must pay off.

People are living longer. Seniors will make up a larger segment of the population than ever before. More retirees, living longer, will create stress on government social services and health care costs.

People are now marrying later in life. They will be faced with having children in college, parents in retirement homes, and their own retirement just around the corner. This is what many call the "sandwich generation" because people are sandwiched between financial goals.

Investments are more numerous but harder to choose. You just can't afford to make mistakes. There are now more mutual funds out there than stocks. How do you choose one?

People are concerned about the economy and terrorism. What impact would another 9/11 have on the stock market?

The picture looks dark and dismal! Where do we find answers?

Don't despair. Many Christians feel that the best financial advice is available to everyone. It is found in the Bible, and it is free!

The Bible, God's word, has excellent advice for all who will hear and follow instructions. The Bible provides guidance about money. It is practical, insightful, and specific. Let's look at it together:

- Jesus told thirty-eight parables—sixteen concerned possessions.

- In Matthew, Mark, and Luke, one out of every six verses addresses the spiritual use of money.

- Search the Bible by topics, and you will find prayer mentioned more than five hundred times, faith mentioned a little less than five hundred times, and material possessions mentioned more than one thousand times.

What does that say to you?

Yes, the Bible gives serious attention to material possessions. Why are material possessions discussed so frequently in the Bible? Why would God discuss it more than prayer? Why is money the most frequently discussed topic in the Bible, with the exception of the kingdom of God?

I believe that how we as Christians reconcile the use of money is the single greatest barrier to our relationship with God. Money is the number one contender for our hearts.

How we handle money seems to be a great challenge for us. It seems to be a character test and an indication of our relationship with God. The way we handle money tells a story about what we believe.

I am reminded of the story that you can know a man's heart by looking at two things in his life: his checkbook and his calendar. It is probably true that how we spend our time and money tells a story of what we believe and what is important to us. It gives an indication of who is in charge of our lives.

The Bible talks a great deal about being a good steward, which means trustee, overseer, or manager. The doctrine of Christian stewardship means the way we as Christians manage God's resources.

So how are we doing? Does society prove "faithful" as God's steward?

2

Is the Church Getting Through?
How are People Doing?

Recently the IRS released statistics concerning 2002 deductions for taxpayers. The study compared the average deductions of home mortgage interest and charitable contributions for different income levels. Here is a summary:

Adjusted Gross Income	Mortgage Interest Expense	Money Given to Charity
$15,000–$30,000	$6,453	$1,890
$30,000–$50,000	$6,850	$2,006
$50,000–$100,000	$8,364	$2,530
$100,000–$200,000	$11,825	$3,875

What do the IRS statistics say about the level of stewardship in this country? What does it say when the average person pays three to five times more in mortgage interest each year than charitable contributions?

I recently saw another set of statistics from the IRS for 2004 that was even worse.

Also, the study did not differentiate between noncash and cash contributions. I would think that a significant portion of the average charitable deduction in the study came from noncash contributions. In other words, people cleaning out their junk and old clothes, deducting an overestimated (probably overstated) value, and giving it to organizations like the Salvation Army.

If Jesus filled out a tax return, what do you thinks his deductions would look like? How much in mortgage interest deductions would he have versus charitable contributions?

What does this study say about the church's stewardship message to the world today? Why is the church not getting through to believers? How do people respond to a biblical message of stewardship? When the church preaches about money, will anyone listen?

In my own experience, when I talk about stewardship to clients who go to church, typically I see three responses to the message:

Response 1: Some people just flat out resent the church's position regarding tithing (giving) and stewardship.

They do not want anybody telling them what they should do with their money. It is their money. They worked hard for it, and the Church should mind its own business. "The church just wants your money."

Tithing often would not even hinder their lifestyles, but they do not recognize that God had anything to do with their successes. They do not think of their own financial blessings as opportunities to honor God. The world is full of rich people that do not feel they owe anybody anything.

People who feel this way are really missing out. This is whom I think Jesus was referring to when he said that it is "easier for a camel to go through the eye of a needle than for a rich person to go to heaven."

For purposes of this text, I am referring to tithing as the biblical teaching that all believers should give 10 percent of their "first fruits" to God through the church. For churchgoing readers of this book, this is not a new concept. Most have heard it before.

Response 2: Some people I talk with agree with the church's position regarding stewardship and tithing but do not feel they are in a position to tithe due to financial pressures.

Their hearts and minds are willing, but debt, high living expenses, and a history of poor spending decisions cause them to believe they are unable to give.

People need to make some tough choices. Obedience to God in tithing often means making a choice not to buy that new car or that bigger house. It means making some tough life changes by saying "no" or "not now." This type of responder must realize the difference between need and want.

The Bible says that when we do not tithe and bring offerings, we are stealing from God. It's ironic that there are so many people in the church who do not tithe, and still they wonder why God is not blessing them. They wonder why there is so much financial pressure in life. They can never get ahead.

It is probably true that they will have difficulty tithing because they have already committed every dollar (and then some) to that bigger house, fancier car, or new beach house. They have bought into the world's view of success and are never satisfied and grateful for what they have. They are more concerned about appearing successful to their neighbors than what God thinks of them. They never experience the joy of giving and meeting the needs of others. It is all about building the lifestyle they want or feel they deserve.

Response 3: The last category of response is from those who are in real financial need. They do not have enough money to meet basic living expenses. They would literally have to borrow to tithe or just go hungry.

It is very difficult to trust God with the first fruits (tithe) when you cannot feed your family. How can you give to the church when you cannot even buy groceries? Sometimes this is because of poor decisions or debt. Sometimes it is just bad luck.

If you are in this category here are two stories to hold on to:

1 Kings 17:12–14

"'As surely as the LORD your God lives,' she replied, 'I don't have any bread—only a handful of flour in a jar and a little oil in a jug. I am gathering a few sticks to take home and make a meal for myself and my son, that we may eat it and die.'

"Elijah said to her, 'Don't be afraid. Go home and do as you have said. But first make a small cake of bread for me from what you have and bring it to me, and then make something for yourself and your son. For this is what the LORD the God of Israel, says: "This jar of flour will not be used up and the jug of oil will not run dry until the day the LORD gives rain on the land."'"

God promises that if you honor him by giving your resources, your "jug of oil" will never run dry. Are you testing his promises in faith? Are you living in faith, proving his promises true?

If you are giving less than 10 percent of your paycheck, start tithing this Sunday. Continue for three months, and see what happens. If you are tithing, this Sunday start giving 15 percent.

Consider this: 10 percent is what God requires. What is the amount of faith you want to live at? Anything above 10 percent is your choice and is considered an offering.

Maybe this will further encourage you. Here is the other story:

I have a friend who was not tithing but knew he should. He started tithing, committing to do it for three months, even though he knew there would not be enough to pay the bills. He tested God in faith, believing that if he tithed, his needs would be met (that is what the Bible says).

The phrase "test him" in Hebrew means "to prove his promises true." Those that have tried it know the truth of this scripture.

He tested God in faith believing that if he tithed, his needs would be met (that is what the Bible says). Here is what happened to my friend.

He had an old, beat-up car and needed a new one. Unfortunately, he could not afford a new one. Every month his car required some repairs. During the three months he tithed, his car did not break down once. The amount he was previously spending on auto repairs (before tithing) was exactly equal to his tithe during those three months.

God does not necessarily provide more and more money in response to giving. He may or may not. But when we are obedient, he promises a blessing.

Think of yourself as a business with shareholders. If people have invested in you to help you start the business and you refuse to pay a dividend out of profits, would they continue to invest in you? How would a shareholder feel if he or she knew that you spent all the business's profits on material things such as that new house or car?

So how do you think God feels about blessing you with financial resources and abilities when you refuse to honor him in tithing? Do you think he would continue to invest in you? Do you think God would continue to buy stock in you?

3

Would God Buy Stock in You?

So why is society not doing better? What are we missing? If we gave a grade to everyone, they would get an F.

In the church, why is it that the same people give most of the money? Why is it most churchgoing people do nothing to further the resources of the church? Why do so few people get the message?

The answer, I believe, is that a lot of people today have an incorrect impression of the church. "They just want your money," many people say. People do not like to be told what to do, especially with their money. They recognize the needs of the church, but they have needs of their own, like kids in college, retirement, parents in a nursing home, that new car, or renovations to the house.

This is a difficult issue for the church, especially when people are in financial need. Church leaders want to be careful not to offend or make someone who is having financial trouble feel guilty. They certainly don't want people to get mad and leave the church because the pastor talks about money.

So does God want your money? What is God's deal with money?

The Bible teaches us some real truths about money. The first truth is that *it is not our money; God owns it.* The Bible teaches that everything we have is a gift from God with the potential to honor him. The only reason we were even created was to glorify God. We are not the owners; God is.

We are his managers—what the Bible calls *stewards*—entrusted with the responsibility of using his resources wisely. God, first and foremost, wants us to recognize his ownership through tithing. Every talent and every thing of value we have exists from God and has the potential to glorify him. He gave us the ability and the opportunity to earn money.

Stewardship, with respect to tithing, is not about us giving 10 percent, but a recognition that God owns 100 percent and allows us to keep 90 percent. The first 10 percent or more goes back to him to support his kingdom (through his church) in recognition of his ownership.

This is not new teaching for most. Most people, however, know this but miss the "why" part.

Why does God want us to give? Why does he want us to recognize his ownership? Why does God want us to make a priority to support his church? Does he must want our money?

Many people recognize that God has blessed them, and they feel motivated to demonstrate that. However, many in the Church believe that their little tithes or gifts won't matter. Their giving is not going to make a difference in the bigger picture of a million dollar plus church budget. They think the church does not need them.

I believe this is sometimes true.

The church probably does not really need them either. Most do not have enough money to really impact the church, especially a larger one.

Back to the main question: is your money really that important to God or to the church? Does God want your money? Why is the Bible so direct about giving or being a good steward? Why does the Bible talk so much about money?

It is easy to see why people get the wrong impression about God and their money.

The answer is that God does not want your money. You don't have enough money that it would matter to him. This is really a heart issue. God wants your giving because he wants your heart. It all goes back to the issue that money seems to be the number one contender for our hearts.

Think about this way; if God needed money, don't you think he could figure out a way to get it? After all, God created the earth. Don't you think if he needed some money to make sure something happened in a church, he could figure out how to get it?

Do you really think people not giving stops God?

So what does he want? What is the connection between the heart and money?

2 Corinthians 9:6–8:

"Remember this: Whoever sows sparingly will also reap sparingly, and whoever sows generously will also reap generously. Each man should give what he has decided in his heart to give, not reluctantly or under compulsion, for God loves a cheerful giver.

"And God is able to make all grace abound to you, so that in all things at all times; having all that you need, you will abound in every good work."

The translation my Dad taught me is: **tithing is not the way God raises money; money is the way God develops Christians**.

When we recognize God's ownership of our financial lives though tithing, we minimize the destructive effects money has on our lives and on our relationships with God.

Money is a dangerous thing. If we don't tame it, it will destroy us. It can easily become what God calls "the root of all evil."

I truly believe all this tithing and stewardship business is for our own good.

Let's look in more detail. The doctrine of stewardship can be found (among other places) in the parable of the talents, found in Matthew 25:14–30:

"Again, it will be like a man going on a journey, who called his servants and entrusted his property to them. To one he gave five talents of money, to another two talents, and to another one talent, each according to his ability. Then he went on his journey.

"The man who had received the five talents went at once and put his money to work and gained five more. So also, the one with the two talents gained two more. But the man who had received the one talent went off, dug a hole in the ground and hid his master's money. After a long time the master of those servants returned and settled accounts with them.

"The man who had received the five talents brought the other five. 'Master,' he said, 'you entrusted me with five talents. See, I have gained five more.' His master replied, 'Well done, good and faithful servant! You have been faithful with a few things; I will put you in charge of many things. Come and share your master's happiness!'

"The man with the two talents also came. 'Master, you have entrusted me with two talents; see, I have gained two more.' His master replied, 'Well done, good and faithful servant! You have been faithful with a few things; I will put you in charge with many things. Come and share your master's happiness!'

"Then the man who had received the one talent came. 'Master,' he said, 'I know you are a hard man, harvesting where you have not sown and gathering where you have not scattered seed. So I was afraid and went out and hid your talent in the ground. See, here is what belongs to you.'

"His master replied, 'You wicked, lazy servant! So you knew that I harvest where I have not sown and gather where I have not scattered seed? Well then, you should have put my money on deposit with the bankers, so that when I returned I would have received it back with interest. Take the talent from him and give it to the one who has ten talents.

"For everyone who has, will be given more, and he will have an abundance. Whoever does not have, even what he has, will be taken from him. And throw that worthless servant outside, into the darkness, where there will be weeping and gnashing of teeth.'"

Not a pretty picture!

Here is a summary of what the parable of the talents teaches us:

1. God is the owner of our financial lives; we are his stewards.

2. God will entrust to us that which is within our ability to manage.

3. God expects multiplication of assets (talents) and not maintenance of assets.

4. Since God is the owner, he has the right to take back what he has given us to manage.

5. Because God owns it all, every spending decision is accountable to him as a spiritual act of worship.

If every act of spending is an act of worship, how can we please God with our use of money? How can we manage our financial affairs in a way that is pleasing to God? How can we best use God-given resources to meet financial needs and desires?

This book in divided into chapters based on principles of biblical financial prosperity. Here is a summary of these principles:

Principle 1: Give to the poor and tithe to show God's ownership and support for God's work.

1 John 3:17

"This is how we know what love is: Jesus Christ laid down his life for us. And we ought to lay down our lives for our brothers. If anyone has material possessions and sees his brother in need but has no pity on him, how can the love of God be in him?"

Proverbs 3:9—10

"Honor the LORD with your wealth, with the first fruits of your crops; then your barns will be filled to overflowing, and your vats will brim over with new wine."

Psalms 24:1

"The earth is the LORD's and all it contains."

Malachi 3:8-10

"But you ask, how do we rob you? In tithes and offerings. You are under a curse—the whole nation of you—because you are robbing me. Bring the whole tithe into the storehouse, that there may be food in my house. Test me in this, says the LORD Almighty and see if I will not throw open the floodgates of heaven and pour out so much blessing that you will not have room enough for it."

2 Corinthians 9:11

"You will be made rich in every way so that you can be generous on every occasion, and through us your generosity will result in thanksgiving to God."

Principle 2: Spend wisely; take care of your family.

1 Timothy 5:8

"If anyone does not provide for his relatives, and especially for his immediate family, he has denied the faith and is worse than an unbeliever."

If we are to honor God with our finances, we must put selfish wants away and provide for our families.

Principle 3: Avoid debt.

Proverbs 22:7

"The rich rule over the poor, and the borrower is servant to the lender."

Simply stated if we are to honor God with our finances, we must stay out of debt.

Principle 4: Save and plan for future needs, emergencies, and goals.

Luke 14:28-30

"Suppose one of you wants to build a tower. Will he not first sit down and estimate the cost to see if he has enough money to complete it? For if he lays the foundation and is not able to finish it, everyone who sees it will ridicule him, saying, this fellow began to build and was not able to finish."

Test: So How Are You Doing?
Take this simple test to open your eyes to areas that need improvement:

1. Are you unhappy because you want something such as a new car or new house?

2. Do you have resentment because you feel that you do not make as much money as others?

3. Do you have debt because you live beyond your means?

4. Do you tithe to your church? Do you give offerings?

5. Do you buy things on impulse or pray about financial decisions?

6. Do you avoid budgets?

If you answered yes to any of these questions, you are struggling with steward-ship.

Bottom line—would God buy stock in you? Will you pay a good dividend? Are you a good risk? Are you a good buy? Will you rise in value? Will you pay your shareholders their portion of the profits?

4

Does God Want You to Financially Prosper?

Before we dive into the biblical principles of success, here is a common question: Does God want us to be financially secure and prosperous? Does he want us to have possessions? The Bible warns us not to lay up treasures here on earth. What exactly does that mean? Does it mean that we should follow the example of Jesus who died on the cross owning nothing?

With all the contrasting poverty and affluence in the world today, it is difficult to know God's plans for us financially. In fact, it is even sometimes hard to believe in God at all.

Jeremiah 29:11

"'For I know the plans I have for you,' declares the LORD, 'plans to prosper you and not to harm you, plans to give you hope and a future.'"

The good news is that God does want us to prosper. The great news is that Jesus came to show us how to have life and have it abundantly.

So if God wants us to prosper, why are so many people in the world starving? On the other hand, why are so many people in the world rich? Does God bless wealthy people? Are they God's favorites? Are they doing something the poor are not? Do they pray more? Do they sin less?

If Christians are wealthy, did God cause that wealth? Does God cause poverty or just handpick some to be wealthy? What about all starving kids in Africa?

The key is to understand the difference between God's system of prosperity and the world's system of prosperity.

It is easy to recognize the world's system of prosperity. The world says that money, success, possessions, and recognition are what we need. You work hard. You deserve that house or car. Feeling down? Go buy a new outfit. You had a long day; let's eat out.

Why not? You and your family deserve the best the world has to offer. God would want it that way.

The world's system of prosperity tells us that we can never have enough and to never be satisfied. Possessions are the basis of fulfillment in life. The world's system tells us to compare ourselves to others because our self-esteems are tied to possessions.

Ecclesiastes 5:10

"Whoever loves money never has money enough; whoever loves wealth is never satisfied with his income. This too is meaningless."

The world's system of prosperity puts "things" ahead of God. God does want us to prosper financially and have abundant life. However, this is true only if this financial prosperity and the things it will buy never in any way come ahead of him. He is first in all things, especially money.

Why does God bless some and not others? I have no idea.

You can ask God when you see him. The real question is not why people are starving. The real question is what to do about it.

We liven in a fallen world. This is especially true here in America. The Bible clearly states that if we see a need, fill it. So in my mind, if we see people in crisis and do not act, we are disobedient.

Remember that the evil one can cause some people to have money as well as God. In fact, there is nothing that I am aware of in the Bible that says that God only causes wealth. That is why I think the Bible talks so much about the subject of money. The repeated warnings are obvious.

Do not feel guilty about having money. If God has blessed you, you have even more responsibility to use your blessings wisely. Fill needs. Remember the parable of the talents and what it teaches. Money can be used for good or evil; it is up to us. Financial disarray is usually of our own creation.

So back to the question of last chapter—if you were a stock, would God invest in you?

Test: Do you have areas that need improvement?

1. How has materialism affected your life? Why is it so hard to live within our means?

2. What does Martha Stewart teach us about the world's system of prosperity?

3. What do Enron, WorldCom, HealthSouth, and other corporate accounting scandals teach us about the world's system of prosperity?

4. Are you truly grateful for what you have, and are you satisfied? Do you acknowledge God for what you have?

5

What Are God's Laws of Prosperity?

In the previous chapter, I suggested that it is easy to feel guilty about having money. It is also easy not to use your financial blessings for good. It is easy to feel egotistical and to not be a good steward. On the other hand, it is easy to be angry for being a have-not.

Wherever you are, consider that the Bible has answers. God gives us laws of prosperity to follow.

Law 1: Put God first.

Matthew 6:33

"But seek first His kingdom and His righteousness, and all these things will be given to you as well."

Deuteronomy 14:23

"Eat the tithes of your grain, new wine and oil, and the first born of your herds and flocks in the presence of the LORD your God at the place He will choose as a dwelling for His Name, so that you may learn to revere the LORD your God always."

Whatever we need in any area of our life, God's law of prosperity says that he will provide to the exact degree that we keep him first in every area of our life. When we keep him first through tithing, we tame the money animal.

Law 2: Give the boss his due.

Deuteronomy 8:18

"But remember the LORD your God, for it is He who gives you the ability to produce wealth, and so confirms His covenant, which He swore to your forefathers, as it is today."

The Bible tells us that everything we have is a gift from God with the potential to honor him. Everything we have—including our money, marriage, children, jobs, brains, and abilities—are gifts that we must choose to honor him. In fact, the Bible says the only reason we are even here is to glorify him.

Law 3: Every act of spending is an act of worship.

It is essential to being a good steward that you view every act of spending as an act of worship to find God's prosperity. What is the good that can come from an act of using money?

Law: 4: We must work using our talents, brains, and backs.

2 Thessalonians 3:10

"For even when we were with you, we gave you this rule: 'If a man will not work, he shall not eat.'"

God wants us to partner with him and not be dependents of Him. We have to do our part. God does not want a bunch of mindless robots; he wants us to actively seek his wisdom in stewardship and be proactive in our financial lives.

People offer suffer from what I call the "ostrich syndrome." What do ostriches do when they sense danger? They stick their heads in the sand, waiting for the danger to pass. Does this sound familiar?

Why do people hide from their financial problems? When do they avoid them?

God gives us time and abilities to use.

What are the barriers to putting God first in your life?

What are the barriers to putting God first in your financial life?

6

First Law of Prosperity—
Putting God First, More Detail

Jesus promised us perfect peace—a total, complete, and absolute peace. Perfect peace certainly includes freedom from financial problems. How can any of us have peace if we worry about financial problems?

So how can we put God first and receive perfect peace? What does that mean?

God has two requirements for perfect peace. We must keep him first at all times. God's law of prosperity will work to the degree that we keep him first in our lives. The blessings we receive will be in direct proportion to the degree we keep him first. Keeping him first means focusing our minds on him at all times and not on our problems.

Secondly, we must trust him completely. We must spend time to find out what the Bible tells us to do, and do it. We must spend the time required to understand God's laws for abundant life and apply them to our own lives.

So how do we do these things?

There are three things that we must do to keep him first in our lives and trust him completely:

1. We must speak his word constantly.

   Joshua 1:8

   "Do not let this Book of the Law depart from your mouth; meditate on it day and night, so that you may be careful to do everything written in it. Then you will be prosperous and successful."

2. We must constantly study his word and meditate on it day and night.

    Psalm 1:1–3

    "Blessed is the man who does not walk in the counsel of the wicked or stand in the way of sinners or sit in the seat of mockers. But his delight is in the law of the LORD, and on his law he meditates day and night. He is like a tree planted by streams of water, which yields its fruit in season and whose leaf does not wither. Whatever he does prospers."

3. We should live our lives exactly as the Bible tells us to.

    The Bible says we show love for God by obeying his commandments.

Test: Do You Put God First in Your Life?

1. Is God always more important to you than friends, family, children, or money?

2. Do you spend more time seeking God each day than watching television?

3. Is God more important than your possessions? Would you give them up if he asked you to?

4. Is seeking God on a daily basis more important to you than seeking financial prosperity?

7

Second Law of Prosperity— Give the Boss His Due

Many Christians wonder why money is so important to God. The reason, I believe, is that money is the number one contender for God's place in our lives. When we tithe, we acknowledge God's ownership by putting him first. Bottom line, the money "animal" is tamed.

The scriptures tell us that when we do not tithe, we steal. Consider this analogy: would you go to the grocery store and steal needed groceries to make ends meet every month?

The beginning point of honoring God in your financial life is for Christians to face up to the fact that it is not *your* money it is God's money. Not giving back to God is stealing.

Is it not ironic that many Christians who don't tithe wonder why they do not receive God's blessings? Think again of yourself as a business with shareholders. If people have invested in you to help you start the business and then you refuse to pay them a dividend out of profits, would they continue to invest in you?

And people wonder why God is not investing and blessing them.

Do you recognize God's hand in your financial life? Do you believe he gave you the ability and opportunity to make money? Do you truly believe money comes from God?

Test of Your Recognition of God's Ownership

1. Are you unhappy because you want something such as a new car or new house?

2. Do you have resentment because you feel that you do not make as much money as others?

3. Do you have debt because you live beyond your means?

4. Are you jealous of others that live in homes in neighborhoods that you would like to live in? Are you jealous of others that have a new car that you have always wanted?

5. Do you tithe to your church?

Test of Your Stewardship

1. Do you buy things on impulse or pray about financial decisions?

2. Do you have a budget?

3. Do you live within your means?

4. Do you have credit card debt?

5. Do you work to learn better ways to manage God's money? Do you seek counsel from professionals and read money management publications?

6. Do you treat every spending and investing decision as a spiritual act of worship?

8

Third Law of Prosperity—
Recognizing Spending as
an Act of Worship that Requires
Effort

Once we recognize God's ownership through tithing, we can focus on our responsibility as stewards to honor God in our spending decisions. We must accept that every act of spending and investing is accountable to God as an act of worship. Biblical financial prosperity means that we manage our financial affairs in such a way that it is pleasing to God. We use God-given resources to meet financial needs and desires.

I find that the reason many do not achieve success in this area is that they are not willing to work. Money management is a spiritual discipline, but it is not easy. Just like a diet or exercising, it requires persistence, commitment, patience, prayer, and dedication.

We need help facing these challenges, and the Bible has help to give. Over one third of Jesus's parables discuss money. The Bible tells us that we cannot separate our finances from our relationship with God. *He is the source of wealth, and we are accountable for how we earn it, spend it, and save it.*

Money management is a spiritual discipline, but it is not easy. Just like a diet or exercising, it requires persistence, commitment, patience, prayer, and dedication.

To give you practical advice that you can use today to improve your situation, the rest of this book is devoted to biblical principles for our financial life. These principles outline how we should use money. Remember good money management does not just happen. You've got to work at it.

Principle 1: Spend wisely; take care of your family.

Principle 2: Avoid debt.

Principle 3: Save and plan for future needs, emergencies, and goals.

Principle 4: Give to the poor and tithe to show God's ownership and support for God's work

9

What Is This Book Really About?
Will It Really Help Me?

If every act of spending is an act of worship, how can we please God with our use of money? How can we manage our financial affairs in such a way so that it is pleasing to God? How can we best use God-given resources to meet financial needs and desires?

This book is divided into chapters based on principles of biblical financial prosperity:

Principle 1: **Give to the poor and tithe to show God's ownership and to support God's work.**

1 John 3:17

"This is how we know what love is: Jesus Christ laid down his life for us. And we ought to lay down our lives for our brothers. If anyone has material possessions and sees his brother in need but has no pity on him, how can the love of God be in him?"

Malachi 3:8–10

"But you ask, how do we rob you? In tithes and offerings. You are under a curse—-the whole nation of you—-because you are robbing me. Bring the whole tithe into the storehouse, that there may be food in my house. Test me in this, says the LORD Almighty and see if I will not throw open the floodgates of heaven and pour out so much blessing that you will not have room enough for it."

2II Corinthians. 9:11

"You will be made rich in every way so that you can be generous on every occasion, and through us your generosity will result in thanksgiving to God."

Malachi 3:10

""'Bring the whole tithes into the storehouse, that there may be food in my house. Test me in this,'" says the LORD Almighty, ""'and see if I will not throw open the floodgates of heaven and pour out so much blessing that you will not have room enough for it.'"

Principle 2: **Spend wisely; take care of your family.**

1Timothy 5:8

"If anyone does not provide for his relatives, and especially for immediate family, he has denied the faith and is worse than an unbeliever."

Principle 3: **Avoid debt.**

Proverbs .22:7:

"The rich rule over the poor, and the borrower is servant to the lender.".

Principle 4: Save and plan for future needs, emergencies, and goals.

Luke 14:28–30

"Suppose one of you wants to build a tower. Will he not first sit down and estimate the cost to see if he has enough money to complete it? For if he lays the foundation and is not able to finish it, everyone who sees it will ridicule him, saying, this fellow began to build and was not able to finish."

10

Spend Wisely—Take Care of Your Family

The first step to spending wisely and being a good steward is gaining control of your cash flow. This step is the easiest to understand and the hardest to implement. It is just flat-out the hardest for people to do.

In order to provide for your family, you must first have discretionary income. From the perspective of a financial advisor, I could teach you everything you need to know to be a wise manager; I could teach you how to invest and avoid taxes, but if you do not have extra income, there is not much I can do to help.

If you have no money what can I really do?

So how can we minimize expenses so that we can save more?

To begin with, I typically like to use an equation:

Income > Outgo (bills)

In other words, what we spend is less than what we earn. If you put a stewardship understanding on the equation, then:

90 percent Income > Outgo

Once you've balanced *this* equation, your job is to use the rest of God's money wisely. Now this is not an easy equation to balance, especially when you have children. However, the bottom line remains—if we commit God's resources to wasteful spending, how can we be financially free to make decisions regarding our families' needs? How can we give as God directs us? God wants us to trust him with our financial life. He wants to partner with us to make smart decisions regarding our resources.

I cannot tell you how many times while in a meeting with a client, I have brought up planning for a goal, such as children's college costs, only to run into barriers because parents are saving for a country club membership or something else as trivial.

What is needed is to minimize expenses and allow for more savings is a system to track expenses and give us accountability for spending. We need help. If you do not know how much you spend and where it is going, how can you plan and take care of your family? How can you plan, save, or give effectively?

Most people (unless you are Paris Hilton), will never have enough today to plan for everything in life. What we need is to balance current assets with current and future needs. A spending plan is not a legalistic set of rules, but an ongoing process of evaluating priorities and setting goals. You must have a method of making decisions based on the reality of what you have, what you need, what you can afford, and where you are going.

Financial freedom is not about how much you earn, but rather consistently earning more than you spend.

A number of software programs out there allow you to organize your spending. People get turned off by the time required to input the information. In reality, a computerized program takes only ten to fifteen minutes per week and actually saves that much time or more when balancing your checkbook, reconciling credit accounts, and organizing for taxes.

Setting up a computerized spending plan:

1. Purchase a program such as Quicken, and install it on your home computer. If you do not have a home computer, see if you can use your office computer during your lunch break or during off-hours.

2. When you write checks for purchases and bills, write down the date, check number, and payee in your check register.

3. Save credit card receipts, and write down the categories of items on the receipt, such as dining out and groceries.

4. Once a week, for approximately ten minutes, input the check register and all receipts information into the computer.

5.   Once a month, run a spending report and evaluate your cash flow.

Once you do this, you will have a handle on cash flow. You can even identify areas to cut waste and start creating a budget. It is that simple.

However, in all my years of being a financial advisor, I have never met anyone who welcomes the idea of sticking to a spending plan or budget. Everyone seems to understand the idea of making a budget, but no one wants to stick with it.

Whenever I talk about it, people tune me out. They are not interested in being lectured about the importance of budgets. They already know that. They think tell me something I do not already know, and can use-like a hot stock tip.

They would much rather I tell them about the investments I recommend, even though they do not have any money to invest.

I have found that only about 5 percent of the people I meet to discuss cash flow issues with will even make the time to do a spending plan. Everyone seems to understand the importance, but most people just do not want to make a change or face the issue.

I am reminded that one of the definitions of insanity is waking up every morning, doing the same thing as the day before but expecting a different result."

Why do people stress themselves out about money every day but at the same time refuse to make any changes?

God can deliver you from theses money burdens. However, you have got to partner with Him and do some work. Get off your butts and deal with money issues in your life.

The solution is simple, a spending plan. Do not whine any more about your finances, if you are unwilling to make a change.

Remember people seem to suffer from "ostrich syndrome." What does an ostrich do when it is afraid? When an ostrich senses danger, it sticks its head in the sand and waits for the danger to leave. This is what people do. They know they have money problems, but instead of facing them, they stick their heads in the sand and hope the danger will leave.

Christians are the worst at this. They believe you should not worry and trust God to provide.

When I ask Christian parents how they are going to pay for college, the response is often, we are praying for a scholarship."

It is not that I do not believe that it is impossible for God to bless you, but in life, most of the time, you have to do some work.

God *can* deliver you from these money burdens. However, you have got to partner with him and do some work. Get off your butts and deal with money issues in your life! God provides opportunities, and we must take advantage.

Parents avoiding their duty to save for their kid's education is obviously one of my pet peeves. Parents, in many cases, have no money saved for college. Because of their parents' lack of discipline, the kids will be paying off student loans for the rest of their lives.

Parents should not leave their children with a legacy of college debt. What an awful way to start off adult life!

The answer that a lot of parents give me is that they trust God to provide. My response is that maybe God has already provided the means, but you just missed it and failed to take advantage.

Do not get me wrong. I am not saying God cannot provide. I am just saying that the majority of the time, you are required to work.

Often God has provided, but instead of saving those resources for some worthy goal like college, you spent it on a new car.

Your kids have a ton of student-loan debt, but you look good to the neighbors!

The least you can do is spend fifteen minutes each week being accountable to God for how you spend his money. I realize that some parents have limited resources and cannot provide for college, but we can all take the time to be a good steward. If you have limited resources, that is all the more reason (not the excuse) to have a spending plan.

It is always interesting to me to hear people's reactions when they ask me the question, "What do you do for a living?" And I say, "I am a financial advisor."

They often respond by saying, "Oh, really? We need to talk to you."

The perception is that I can offer a "magic pill" that will make all their financial problems go away—kind of like a diet pill that allows you to eat whatever you want, never exercise, and lose all the weight required to make you a Victoria's Secret model.

Bottom line—I never met anyone who welcomed the idea of living on a budget or spending plan.

Knowing how tough this is for everyone and how important it is to all potential planning, here are some motivations that should help:

1. The Bible teaches that we are stewards entrusted with God's resources and accountable for how we use them. How can you be accountable to God if you do not know where your money is going and you do not have a spending plan?

2. Do you know of any corporations or businesses that do not keep track of expenditures and use that information for planning purposes? Would you buy stock in a company that did not?

3. The only time in the Bible that God says, "Test me," is in regards to stewardship. He promises blessings for faithfulness.

Think of the importance of this last item. This is the only time I am aware of in the entire Bible that God says that we can test him. This is the only time in the Bible that he allows this.

I believe that God knows how difficult this is in our lives. I think he is trying to give us extra motivation. It goes back to this issue of money being the number one contender for God's place in our lives.

So here is the rest of the list:

4. How would you like to eliminate the stress of keeping up with how much money you have available in your accounts and when the bills are due? Do you have fear of missing important due dates or wonder where the money is going to come from to make the payments?

5. Do you get "credit card surprise" when the bill is received because of the amount charged on it? Would it not be easier just to go to the computer and see an accumulated total of purchases so you are prepared before the bills are due?

6. Do you need to save? Do you want to pay off your credit cards monthly? How can you do that without knowing discretionary cash flow? The only way to know discretionary income is with a spending plan.

Again the bottom line is unless you have enough money each month to spend freely, you need a spending plan.

Furthermore, if you have that much money that you can spend without limits, you are not a good steward without a plan. You are wasting God's resources.

11

Avoid Debt—How Can You Do It?

Borrowing is not expressly forbidden in scripture, but it is repeatedly warned against, particularly in Proverbs. "The borrower is servant to the lender," cautions Proverbs 22:7.

Why does God discourage debt? One obvious reason is the bondage that comes with debt, both financially and emotionally. Debt presumes on the future and on God. If our resources are precommitted because of past credit use, we cannot be financially free to give as God directs us.

In other words, if you are spending every dime on debt payments, it is safe to say you are not tithing.

The reality of modern life is that people are burdened by debt and cannot save. The world allows us to overspend. So here is the real question: if we want to honor God with our finances, how can we avoid debt?

In the previous chapter, I discussed the importance of having a spending plan to avoid debt. This is the starting place. Without a spending plan, everything else is a waste of time. From a stewardship standpoint, if you want to be obedient to God as a steward, a spending plan is essential.

In this and the next few chapters, I want to focus on specific ways that we can reduce expenditures, eliminate debt, and promote discretionary savings.

Many books of this type offer great advice but no means to get control of your situation. Many books start out with advice such as how you should pay off all credit cards and save 10 percent of your income.

With what—did you win the lottery?

This is good advice but not very practical for the real world when you are in debt or have kids (the endless money pit).

The goal of the following chapters is not to provide some "pie in the sky" recommendations. *My* goal is to tell you how you can eliminate waste and get out of debt.

What most people need is practical advice that meets them where they are today. By the way, this stuff is not rocket science; however, people still miss it.

The first idea is to replace your current credit cards with a lower rate and get a rebate card. When you restructure your credit cards, you can reduce interest costs and speed up repayment. You will get out of debt quicker.

A rebate card is cash back bonus card. The bank pays you a percentage of expenditure either monthly or annually.

If you will fully utilize lower rate, rebate credit cards, you can save thousands of dollars each year. This just puts money in your pocket that you can use to pay off more debt.

I have told people that if they would just get a rebate cards and invest the money they receive, they could provide for about one to two years of college expenses for at least one child. What a great college savings plan!

What could be easier?

The beauty of the idea is that you did not have to do anything. Just use a rebate card to make purchases like you normally would.

Why do people not switch a current credit card to a lower rate card?

You would think this is common sense. It does not seem so. Every day I am amazed at how much people are paying in interest.

Check out www.bankrate.com. This is a great source for rebate cards and research on available interest rates for loans and cards.

The goal here is to match a rebate card with lower rate cards that meets your needs, and creates spending discounts.

For example, if you are a new parent, you can find cards that offer substantial rewards for purchasing products that you are going to buy anyway, like diapers. The key is to look for rebate cards the offers discounts on products that you already purchase. Why not save 25 percent on diapers or formula? It is possible.

Another example might be to use a gas rebate card if you have to drive for a living—or even for everyone else. Suppose you could save 5–10 percent on gas every week. At today's gas prices, this could add up.

Why not use a rebate card to buy gifts for Christmas or to buy office supplies if you own your own company? Why not use it for every purchase? It is free, tax-free money!

Many people ask me if they should use teaser rates or an equity line on their house to pay off debt. This is a good way to lower interest costs to eliminate debt; however, here is a word of caution. Check the fine print. Many teaser rate cards or loans have above-average minimum payments and very high rates after the initial teaser rate period.

If you decide to switch to another card, be careful about these questions. Ask them before signing up: Does the new card have fraud protection against others using (stealing) my card? Do you charge a fee for moving the balance?

Another idea to look into before switching a card with a lower rate is to negotiate with your current credit card company to receive a lower rate on existing cards. Give them a call and the opportunity to lower your rate. Explain that if they do not match or better the new rate, you are switching.

As far as consolidating with an equity line, I am actually in favor of this if you can do the analysis correctly. I will get to that in a moment.

Here is a trick question. Answer carefully:

> Suppose you are five years into a thirty-year mortgage loan at 7 percent and owe $150,000.

Should you refinance your loan if you are offered a 6.25 percent thirty-year-fixed rate that would cost you $2,000 and drop your payment $74 a month?

Most people believe that they would break even in 2–2.5 years. Meaning that if you divided the closing costs ($2000) by the $74 savings per month, it would take around twenty-four months to break even.

In other words, if you spent $2000 up-front to refinance, then at a savings of $74 each month, it would take around two years to get your money back (27 months x $74).

So what do you think? Here are the numbers:

Current Loan	7 percent	Refinanced Loan	6.25 percent
Remaining Years	25	Remaining Years	30

So if you are going to stay in the house for a few years, it makes sense to refinance. Right?

Wrong—the correct answer is that you should *not* refinance!

The reason for the payment savings is because you are extending your loan five more years.

With the current loan being five years old, you need to calculate the break-even point using twenty-five years, not thirty. The trick is to calculate the savings over the remaining period of the loan. If you calculate the break-even over twenty-five years, it only saves you eight dollars per month. Therefore, it would take twenty years to recoup the costs.

The point is that you must compare cash flow payments to determine the interest savings. More often, the appearance of savings comes from extending the loan repayment period, not from a reduced interest rate.

Most people would have said yes to the refinance because the payment dropped seventy-four dollars.

It drives me nuts when I hear TV or radio ads that talk about how consolidating debts saved the person so much money each month. Rubbish! More often the appearance of monthly payment savings is *not* due to the rate reduction but from extending the consolidation loan out over a longer repayment period. You may lower the monthly payment but end up paying more over the life of the loan.

There is nothing wrong with consolidating debt, but be clear as to the savings. If it is not due to the rate reduction you should not do it.

You must compare cash flow payments over the same period to determine the interest savings. Compare the repayment over the same term to see what influence the rate reduction has on the repayment of interest.

You must calculate the total amount repaid. For example:

Suppose you owe $10,000 of debt at 10 percent and have a monthly payment of $900 a month. It would take you around one year to repay the loan. The total repayment over the year would be $10,548. Therefore you would pay $548 of interest.

Consider if you were offered a new loan at 6 percent at a payment of $750 per month. The total amount repaid is over about a year. This would actually save you. Plus, the lower monthly payment would free up some cash.

Worth doing—you bet!

Suppose the consolidation loan was offered at 8 percent and a payment of $250 per month. Most people would think this is great because their payment dropped $650 a month. Rubbish!

Will this loan take longer than a year to repay? You bet.

I throw in this example because for years I have taught a financial class at my church and asked this question. Never in all those years did I get anyone to give me the correct answer. The problem is that we are smart enough to figure this out; however, we are programmed toward monthly payments, not the total cost over the life of the loan.

This is why I believe the first word out of the car sales person's mouth is, "What are you looking to spend? How much can you afford each month?"

This is why in almost every ad on TV; cost is quoted in terms of a payment instead of total cost. You never hear, "You can own this dining room table for two thousand dollars."

Advertisers sell you on the fact that you can own this table for no payments for a whole year and just five bucks a month. Wow, just five dollars a month! We can afford that!

Of course they never mentioned that the table eventually cost you $7000 for a $5000 table because you are paying on the loan for the next ten years.

I am not saying that you should never use financing, but have a brain when looking at this. Do not end up a slave to payments because you have made purchases in the past and are still paying for them.

I am not saying that everything you buy should be in cash. However, realize what happens when you string out purchases over a long period.

To make matters even worse, people do this when buying items that lose value from use every year (like cars)—this is called *depreciation*. At least do this with items that grow in value like a house.

As for equity lines, I am in favor of consolidating debts with an equity line even though an equity line rate often is variable. Meaning the can change. Many people shy away from this because of that fact. People could be saving a lot of money in interest by using equity lines.

Consider this: if the biggest negative to consolidating debt with a home equity loan is having a variable rate, then what about credit cards? I agree it is a negative, but credit cards also have variable rates. Both types of debt are based on the prime rate; however, an equity line is usually deductible at least up to one hundred thousand dollars of principal. Most people realize that because you can write interest off your taxes, it lowers your eventual cost.

Furthermore, you generally will receive better rates over the long run because an equity line is secured to your house. The bank has greater security of repayment than an unsecured credit card; therefore, they offer you a better rate.

Where I differ is when the banks charge a lot of closing costs. Most equity lines are free. There are no costs. If your bank wants to charge you closing costs, go somewhere else.

Also, I would not recommend paying off a car loan because a car loan term is shorter (it pays off faster) and the rate is fixed and usually lower than a line of credit. This is also true of student loans. Student loans may even be deductible in some situations.

Also, from time to time banks offer teaser rates on equity lines or fixed rates for some period of time. Take advantage.

This one would be good idea to run past your CPA or advisor before moving ahead.

Bottom line—when you take advantage of lower rates, especially deductible ones like a home equity loan, you can pay off your debts sooner. This, coupled with a rebate card, helps you get out of debt. Once out of debt, you can save effectively.

This chapter may be common sense to most, but be careful about messing up the analysis. Get help if you need it. Remember Proverbs—do not be a slave.

Another word of caution: I hesitate to bring up any of these ideas in this chapter because of potentially negative results. Many people consolidate debts only to spend more. Once they put all their debts together in one low payment, even if it makes sense, they just go out and run up the cards again. The assumption is that you are going to be diligent and aggressive in paying off your debts.

If these ideas are going to tempt you to go out and run up the cards some more, do not consolidate or switch cards.

12

Avoid Debt, Part 2—Restructuring and Reducing Auto Purchases

Outside of a home purchase, an automobile is typically the most expensive and necessary purchase you will make. This is especially true in cities, like mine, where public transportation is not very good. I realize many cities have public transportation that can potentially save you a lot of money by making owning a car less of a necessity.

People waste more money buying cars! I am amazed when people spend as much on their cars as they do on their houses. How stupid! People many times do not give a second thought to how much money they spend on cars. Because of this, a lot of opportunity is missed to save for other goals.

What is more important: driving that new car or sending your kids to college?

This chapter is entirely devoted to how consumers can reduce the cost of a car. If we can reduce these costs, we can be better able to pay off debt and reach other goals.

The first question that always comes up is, "Should I buy or lease?"

Bottom line—if you do not replace a car frequently and keep them for the long haul, leasing is almost always more expensive than buying even when you consider maintenance costs.

One possible exception is when using an automobile for business use because it is tax deductible. This is beyond the scope of this book. Talk to your CPA to understand planning for this area.

The cheapest way to own a car will always be to buy a used car two to three years old or older and drive it until the wheels fall off. It is stupid to trade in an older car because it is out of warranty or because you are maintaining it. Consider how much a new car costs.

A new car will never cost less than maintaining an older car.

The biggest mistake people make, regardless of car type, is getting sucked into the monthly payment mentality. In my opinion, the main reason dealers push leasing is because the payments are lower than purchasing. Leasing is less expensive in the short run but more expensive in the long run.

Do not lease! Leasing is a complex transaction that few people will be able to understand.

In my opinion the only ones who really benefit for leasing are the self-employed. If you are in the minority, and own your own business, get help from your CPA before committing.

In my experience, the best way to save money on a car and reduce debt is to know the numbers before visiting the dealer. Check out www.edmonds.com or www.kbb.com (Kelly Blue Book) for invoice prices, trade-in values, the cost of extras, and estimated depreciation. These Web sites are great; use them.

I know from personal experience that if you just know what the new car purchase price should be and how much you should receive for a trade-in, then you can save a lot of money. Knowing this will help you negotiate and get the best deal.

Common sense, right?

It isn't ironic that whenever someone buys a car they always say they got a great deal. People say "I got the best deal." The dealers are just giving the cars away! What a charity! They must be a not-for-profit business.

My belief is the average consumer will not even know if he or she got a good deal or was taken advantage of, unless you know the numbers.

If you rely on the salesman to explain what a deal you received, you are in trouble. If you think that since the car salesperson is nice or goes to your church and you did not question him on the numbers, you are in trouble. You just paid too much.

If you believe the salesman when he tells you that he cannot go any lower on the price or give you more money for your trade, you are in trouble.

Sometimes being willing to walk away is all you need to do to get your price. I know people do not like to haggle with the dealers, but unless they do, they are going to pay for it.

Be informed. Believe the numbers of a third party research firm like Kelly Blue Book, not the car salesman.

Knowing those numbers will tell you what you should pay for the car. Knowing this, you can negotiate confidently.

Besides being an informed consumer when car shopping, consider these ideas:

Use the potential insurance costs as a guide before buying. This makes up 15–20 percent of the total annual cost of a car. Consider the fact that insurance can be as much as your payment. For most people, car insurance is an afterthought. Many people call their auto insurance agents from their cell phones while driving home with the new car.

Insurance premiums vary widely depending on the type of car you drive. Insurance should influence your choice of automobile. Also, available on the above Web sites are detailed calculations of the cost of owning a particular car. You can find information such as maintenance costs for new tires and oil changes, and other costs like gas mileage and car loss of value. Knowing these numbers will help you further narrow your selection.

Many cars in the same price range have very different monthly costs. Choose wisely. Why not let this guide your buying decision? Do not just fall in love with some car that you have to have. Get the numbers.

One common question is what to do for the sake of the safety of children. If keeping an older car and saving the car payment is the pathway to riches, what should you do if that older car is no longer dependable?

I do not recommend you lease; however, if you cannot afford a new car and there is a safety risk with your old one, you may need to lease one car that is dependable and safe for transporting children and own one older car to reduce costs.

While it is easy to tell people never to lease, the reality is that cars are expensive. People are going to buy new cars. This is true whether or not they understand the loose of value of a new car versus old. Many people needing a new car must lease to afford the payments. It may not be smart, but people will do it anyway.

As a parent, I am not about to stick my wife with an old clunker, driving my kids everywhere. The men should drive the clunker. The wife and kids should have the new, safe car.

Furthermore, if you choose to lease, then understand what you are doing. Find cars with the least amount of depreciation over the term of the lease (check edmonds.com, kbb.com).

When people lease a car they are usually too mindful of the payments and base their decisions on this solely. To make matters worse, the dealers know this and tinker with the lease numbers.

There are three factors that influence the cost of a lease:

Capitalized Cost	- Purchase Price
Residual Value	- Buyback Price (price to own the car at the end of the lease)
Lease Factor	- Interest Rate

If you lease be careful. Here are some things to look out for:

Be careful that a lease does not have an inflated purchase price that is used to calculate the monthly payments. This could be higher than the actual price you would pay to buy the car outright. This easily happens because people focus on payment and not the total cost of the car. When you negotiate, ask for the best price based on paying cash and then tell the salesperson you may want to lease.

Do not accept it when the salesperson tells you the cash price is not available for a lease and that the lease price is higher. If necessary, go to an independent lease company. This is a company that does not sell you the car but make their money by leasing one to you. They do not care what the car costs as long as it is realistic.

Also, dealers often make as much on financing the vehicle. Be prepared not to use dealer financing.

In fact, you may want the leasing company to negotiate for the car directly instead of going through the dealer. Many times an independent company will shop around and receive a better price than you can. They could care less what the purchase price is or markup is. They will merely buy the car on your behalf and lease it back to you.

You might want to visit the dealer for a test drive, but in the end, visit the leasing company.

Furthermore, many times dealers ask you to pay for a lot of options you do not need or want. This is because of low dealer inventory. An independent company may have to get your exact car from the factory or from out of state. Do not get caught paying more because the dealer did not offer you what you want. Do not pay for options you do not need.

Dealers often greatly inflate residual value—or buyback price—to lower monthly payments, but at the end of the lease you usually end up paying more than what the car is actually worth. Your residual value should be no higher than the whole-sale or trade-in price at that time.

Dealers are not required to disclose the effective Annual Percentage Rate (APR) on a car loan; you must learn how to calculate the cost of money.

Instead, a dealer may disclose only the lease factor, also called the lease rate or money factor, which is a much lower number. It is used to calculate the interest portion of the monthly lease payment. Multiply the lease factor by twenty-four to figure out the real interest rate.

Example: A lease factor of five is 0.005. So the actual interest rate is 0.005 x 24, or 12 percent.

I could write a whole book about leasing. The most important thing to remember is: when you lease cars, lease the cars that have the best resale value at the end of the lease.

I expect some people reading this chapter will stare into space saying they could never do all this! This stuff saves thousands. Talk to your CPA or advisor about this if you have questions.

I know that is seems easier to just go buy the car you want and not pay attention to any of this. But, do you want to get out of debt?

13

Avoiding Debt, Part 3—Miscellaneous Tips

Tip: Many people have student loans and need to consolidate them.

Certainly parents should make every effort to send their kids to college, but student loans are a reality of life. With rates very low these days, you can reduce your student-loan payments and pay off the loan early. Many people miss this opportunity to lower the cost of the loan through consolidation.

There are three main sources of consolidation. Check them out online:

1. The Collegiate Funding Service (www.cfsloans.com)

2. Sallie Mae (www.salliemae.com)

3. The Government Direct Loan program (www.loanconsolidation.ed.gov)

There are also other ways to reduce costs.

Making education loan payments electronically from a bank account saves the time and the hassle of writing and mailing checks. Lenders like it too because with timely automatic payments, they have lower loan administration costs.

Some lenders offer rate reductions for paying electronically. For example, Sallie Mae's Direct Repay program can reduce the interest rate on most education loans they service by one-quarter of a percentage point. Others do this as well.

Paying education loans on time helps borrowers maintain excellent credit records and can save money too. Some lender's offer rate reductions or account credits for timely payments. Sallie Mae offers several programs to reward borrowers who pay on time. They further reduce your rate.

I am discouraged by the lack of parents' commitment to save for their kids' college educations. Most parents could avoid sticking their kids with loans to pay off for twenty years after school. They just need to make some hard choices, buckle down, and save.

I am sure some parents reading this will be upset by my comments; however, I seriously doubt all parents who have student loans for their kids' college costs have done everything they could have done to provide for their children's educations. Why could they not wait on that new car?

My apologies to parents who have done everything they could but still have to get loans.

By the way, for the Christian readers of this book, "praying for scholarships" is not an excuse for spending needed college savings on stupid stuff.

Tip: Eliminate PMI from your mortgage.

If you own a home, at the time of purchase if you incurred PMI (Private Mortgage Insurance), you may be able to reduce your payment.

PMI has always meant homeowners can buy a home sooner for less money down. This is a good thing, not a rip-off like everyone says. Without it, many people would not be able to get a loan.

Federal law assures consumers they can enjoy the benefits of PMI knowing that lenders will cancel it when it is no longer needed. However, homeowners are more confused than ever as to when it can be canceled.

Here are the rules:

1. Lenders must send borrowers an annual reminder that they have PMI and have the right to request cancellation once they have met cancellation requirements. This requirement applies to all loans with cancelable PMI.

2. For most loans originated on or after July 29,1999, a lender must cancel PMI at the request of a borrower whose mortgage balance is 80 percent of the original value of the house. The borrower must be up-to-date on mortgage payments and have no other loans on the house (including equity lines). The lender must be satisfied that the property value has not declined.

3. For most loans originated on or after July 29, 1999, PMI will be canceled automatically when the mortgage balance is at 78 percent of the original value of the house. The borrower must be up-to-date on mortgage payments. Otherwise, insurance will be canceled automatically once the borrower becomes current.

What determines if a loan meets cancellation requirement?

Answer these questions to see if you might qualify for PMI cancellation:

*   Have I paid down my mortgage to 80 percent loan to value?

*   Have I made structural improvements that will increase the value of my home?

*   Have homes in my neighborhood appreciated significantly in value?

If you answer yes to these questions, you may be able to cancel your PMI.

Contact your loan servicer using the information provided on your monthly coupon or invoice. Explain to your servicer that you are interested in canceling your PMI and request information on their cancellation requirements.

Meet any requirements provided by your servicer. These may include:

*   Supplying information on property improvement

*   Having an appraisal

*   Sending a request in writing for cancellation of PMI

A note of caution: the company you make your payment to needs to arrange for the appraiser. If you do it yourself or use an appraiser not approved by the company, you may end up paying for two appraisals.

Tip: Choose the right mortgage for that new house or when refinancing your loan.

Choosing the right type of home loan will save you thousands. The type of loan that is right for you (ARM, fixed, points) depends on how long you are going to live in the house. The focus is not always on a lower payment or rate but the interest savings over the period of time you will remain in the home.

Look at the next example. You will notice that each loan has a different closing cost structure. The higher the up-front cost, the lower the rate.

		Loan 1	Loan 2	Loan 3	Loan 4
1st	Loan Amount	$200,000.00	$200,000.00	$200,000.00	$200,000.00
	Interest Rate	6.375%	6.625%	6.875%	7.125%
	Term (months)	360	360	360	360
	Payment	$1,248	$1,281	$1,314	$1,347

Totals		Loan 1	Loan 2	Loan 3	Loan 4
	Total Payment	$1,248	$1,281	$1,314	$1,347
	Monthly Savings (Before-tax)	$100	$67	$34	$0

Months to Compare: 72	Loan 1	Loan 2	Loan 3	Loan 4
Total Payment	$89,837	$92,205	$94,598	$97,015
Principal Paid	$16,195	$15,549	$14,922	$14,316
Interest Paid	$73,642	$76,656	$79,675	$82,699
Balance Left	$183,805	$184,451	$185,078	$185,684
Closing & Pts.	$4,000	$2,000	$2,000	$0
Total Cost over 7 years	$77,642	$78,656	$81,675	$82,699
Net savings	$5,057	$4,043	$1,024	$0

So how do you choose a loan? Consider a simpler example:

Which is Better?	0% Origination Fee 0% Discount Points	1% Origination Fee Typical bank loan
Loan Amount	$150,000	$150,000
Interest Rate	7.25%	7.00%
Principal & Interest Payment	$1,049	$1,023
Cost of Origination Fee	**$0**	**$1,500 (1% of loan amount)**
Interest Paid Over 72 Months	$63,159	$60,890
Total Cost = (Interest Paid + Fees)	$63,159 + 0 $63,159	$60,890 + 1,500 $62,390
Net Savings Before Tax Deductions	$0	$769 This is actually less of a savings when you consider the interest deduction.
Net Savings After Tax Deduction Assuming the 30% Tax Bracket	$0	$538

Most mortgage companies and banks charge origination fees and points. Typically their rates will be 1/8–1/4 percent lower than a loan without origination fees or discount points. While your payment is lower, the closing costs are higher.

The focus should not be on a lower payment, but the interest savings over the period of time you will remain in the home, versus the cost to close the new loan.

Over six years, the lower rate only saved you $538. Why are you giving up the use of $1,500 to save $538?

Why not use that money to reduce the mortgage, invest in a mutual fund, or pay off a credit card? If you invest the origination fee and earn 5 percent after tax, it could grow to $2,127 in seventy-two months, which is much greater than what you saved from the lower rate.

The key is to design the mortgage to account for the period of time you plan to remain in the home. *Unless you know you will remain in the home for a long period of time, you should never pay an origination fee or discount points.* Most people move every five to seven years. So why pay the fees for a lower rate?

In addition to paying costs, you should decide between a fixed and an adjustable rate mortgage (ARM).

The fixed-rate mortgage is the most popular and, in many cases, the best choice. The interest rate remains constant over the life of the mortgage.

With an adjustable-rate mortgage, the interest rate is not guaranteed to remain level over the life of the loan. The interest rate will be guaranteed for some period of time, such as one, three, five, seven, or ten years and then "adjusts" to a market rate. Because an adjustable mortgage interest rate is usually lower than a fixed rate during the guaranteed period, it may save you thousands of dollars in interest.

Consider the following examples:

John and Peggy's starter home is comfortable. However, they plan to start a family and move into another school system within five years. They should consider a five- or seven-year adjustable-rate mortgage because of the lower interest rate.

Jim and Betty built their dream home and plan to stay there until retirement. They should consider a thirty-year fixed mortgage. This type of loan has less risk. They also should consider paying off the mortgage sooner than thirty years with a fifteen-year (or less) mortgage to save interest over the life of the loan.

The most common mistake people make is that they choose the type of mortgage, fixed or adjustable, without considering how long they will be in the house. People choose the fixed rate even though they will only be there five years, or the adjustable rate because the payment is lower, or even worse, an interest-only loan.

It goes without saying that if people would just think the mortgage decision through, they would save thousands of dollars.

14

Avoid Debt, Part 4—Buy the Right Kind of Life and Disability Insurance

Probably the most frequent area of advisor abuse I see is in the area of insurance. People seem to spend a lot of money on insurance for the right reasons but buy the wrong policies from their agents. In addition, there seems to be a lot of misinformation by the agent in an effort to make a sale.

So how can you save money while protecting your family?

The starting point is to determine how much life insurance coverage you need, what type, and where to get it. The goal here is to reduce expenses.

Consider this work sheet:

Minimum Coverage Needed	**= Immediate Cash Needs + Income Replacement**
Immediate Cash Needs	+ Income Replacement
+ Burial Expenses	Annual Pretax Income Needed
+ College Savings (Today's Cost)	X Number of Years of Maximum Income Needed
+ Consumer debt	

Example

$10,000 Burial	$40,000 Income Needed
+ $25,000–$5,000	x 10 Years
+ $5,000 Debt	
$35,000	+ $435,000

Minimum Coverage Needed = $435,000

Now that you can determine some reasonable amount of coverage, you must decide on the type of insurance to purchase. There are two types of insurance: term insurance and cash value insurance.

Term insurance, as the name implies, is for a specified period. It is pure coverage only. Cash value insurance has an insurance portion and an investment portion.

Here is an example:

	Ten-Year Level Term Policy		Cash Value Policy	
Year	Annual Premium	Policy Cash Value	Annual Premium	Policy Cash Value
1	300	0	1,500	0
2	300	0	1,500	0
3	300	0	1,500	2,000
4	300	0	1,500	3,500
5	300	0	1,500	7,500
6	300	0	1,500	11,000
7	300	0	1,500	12,000
8	300	0	1,500	15,000
9	300	0	1,500	19,000
10	300	0	0	22,000
11	5,000	0	0	25,000
12	7,500	0	0	27,000

Observations: Term insurance allows for maximum amount of coverage for the least amount of premium over a limited time. In this example it costs five times less but is only affordable for ten years. Cash value insurance costs more initially, but the extra premium accumulates cash value and can be used to pay premiums in the later years, or it can be used for other goals such as college or retirement.

So how do you decide which is better? The key issue is: what will be your future insurance needs?

One argument against term insurance is that it is for a specified period of time. Later in life, term insurance can become unaffordable. Cash value life insurance can provide permanent protection for later in life.

However, as you build assets and wealth, your dependents will have greater ability to replace lost income from saved assets, and less insurance is needed to bridge the time period until those assets can be accumulated.

My apologies to the insurance agents out there as I know they will not be happy with this chapter.

Many agents will argue that you should buy insurance for when you will need it. Cash value insurance accounts for the majority of claims because it is the only insurance most people keep late in life. Term insurance is unaffordable late in life.

They will dispute that your insurance needs in the future demand cash value insurance especially due to estate taxes or retirement needs. They will also argue that there is a better rate of return with variable life insurance. They will slam the idea of buying term insurance and investing the difference, and insurance is a great way to invest because of tax avoidance.

What you will hear is actually a good argument, but the real issue is priorities. When you need insurance is when your family is dependent on you.

The problem I have with agents is they end up many times selling cash vale insurance instead of term insurance. To me it does not really matter that you need insurance latter in life. By then, you should have the assets and not even need it. When you need it is when your family is dependant on you.

Often people spend so much on cash value coverage that they do not have adequate coverage.

As a general rule, especially if you are a parent, I teach the following regarding insurance planning priorities:

Insurance Planning Priorities—Buy needed protection first, accumulation next:

- Do not even consider cash value insurance if you lack discretionary income for insurance purchases. The first priority is to own term life insurance coverage that you need to protect your family today. The issue is not what happens when you are eighty, but what happens today. What happens to your family if something happens to you today?

- Once your coverage needs are met through term insurance and before considering cash value insurance, you should satisfy other minimum insurance needs such as disability, home, auto, etc.

- Once other non-life insurance needs are met and before considering cash value insurance, you should focus on paying off all credit card debt and have a savings account, or at a minimum, access to three months of living expenses through a home equity loan to meet emergencies.

- Once all three priorities have been met, cash value insurance should be evaluated as an investment choice together with IRAs, 401(k), mutual funds and other alternatives. Choose the best investment for your situation. Get help from your CPA if needed.

In Summary:

Priority 1:	Right mount of life insurance coverage
Priority 2:	Right amount of non-life insurance coverage—especially disability insurance
Priority 3:	Pay off credit cards and create liquidity for emergencies
Priority 4:	Evaluate all available investment options

So if you agree with me that most people should buy term insurance, where do you find it?

Many agents will not recommend this type of insurance. I believe the reason is commissions. I know agents will tell you this is not true. In the previous example, the commission for term insurance would be about $350 versus whole life, which would be $1200. Which do you think most agents will recommend? You want to tell me this does not matter to the agent? They would have to sell four term policies for every one cash value policy.

There are numerous sites on the Internet that provide term insurance comparisons. Once you have determined your needs, you can quickly search for the lowest costs.

Most insurance agents have access to a number of companies as well, even outside their primary company. This is true even though they may be with a company like New York Life.

In general, you will not pay more for coverage by purchasing the insurance through a local agent; however, you will typically pay more if you buy insurance through the agent's primary company.

Policies that pay commissions to agents in general are not more expensive than those from direct companies; therefore, I would recommend that you discuss coverage with your agent or an agent recommended to you by a friend, but buy the right type of coverage. If your agent refuses to discuss term policies, find a new agent.

Employer-provided insurance plans and trade associations provide an excellent and inexpensive option for purchasing insurance as well. You should take advantage of this. They are typically offered at lower costs.

However, a note of caution: because employers can change plans or you may change jobs, you should have a balance of coverage between employer-provided and individual coverage. Take advantage of the cost savings at work but have outside coverage as well that you own and control.

Many times people ask me how to find insurance if they have health concerns and are possibly uninsurable.

You would be surprised to find that many companies will underwrite less than perfect health histories. Check with your insurance agent. Most will be able to do a preliminary inquiry in which they request your medical history be sent to multiple insurers for offers. Offers can then be evaluated for competitive premiums.

Term insurance is appropriate for almost everyone. Even people in their sixties can find good rates these days. Due to intense competition among life insurance companies, consumers find that many policies cost less than half of what they did six or seven years ago.

Even if you bought a policy as recently as two or three years ago, you may be able to save at least 10 percent by trading it in for a new policy. This is an especially good idea if you lost weight, stopped smoking, or got off high blood pressure medication since you bought your last policy.

Once you have some possibilities, you should narrow your choice by looking at some features, such as conversion options and ratings.

Look for conversion options that can be used. If your needs change, a conversion option allows your policy to be converted into a cash value policy later without medical underwriting regardless of your current health history. Also, look at the financial ratings of the issuer. You should only consider top companies.

When looking for coverage, what type of term insurance should you buy?

There are two types of term insurance: annual renewable terms and level premium terms. Annual renewable terms cover you for a twelve-month period. They charge premiums that increase every year. To make the arrangement more affordable, companies typically charge lower rates during the first few years and then sharply increase the premiums after that.

Level-premium terms charge the same fixed annual premiums for set periods, usually five, ten, fifteen, or twenty years. Even though their initial premiums are usually higher than those for annual renewable terms, level-term policies usually cost less over a specific term.

Here is an example:

Example

Year	Annual Renewable	Level Term
1	300	400
2	320	400
3	350	400
4	400	400
5	490	400
6	600	400
7	680	400
8	800	400
9	1000	400
10	1200	400
Total Paid	6,140	4,000

Most people will save money by purchasing level-term policies that match the period of maximum coverage need (i.e., when kids are out of college). Here are some simple steps to follow when buying term insurance:

1. Determine the amount of coverage (see previous work sheet).

2. Determine the period of coverage needed. The period needs to be the time period of maximum coverage needs (i.e., time until children are grown).

3. Compare guaranteed premiums for policies over the period of maximum coverage needed.

4. Narrow the field by comparing financial strength of the company, conversion options, and price and underwriting guidelines.

Now it is time to spend a little of your money. Often people overlook the area of disability insurance and avoid the coverage.

So how do you decide if you need disability insurance?

Answer: if your income stopped today, would you be able to pay your bills from saved assets? If an illness or injury would leave you with insufficient cash to pay your bills, you should consider buying disability insurance.

Many people will respond by saying they have employer-provided disability insurance, so they do not need any more. While it is true that many people are covered by an employer's disability policy, this coverage is often a taxable benefit when received and very limited. In such cases, it is advisable to supplement your coverage.

Maybe this example will help:

Suppose you need $4,000 per month to cover bills (annual budget need = $48,000).

Your employer provides 60 percent coverage. Because your employer pays the premium or you payroll deduct the cost of coverage using pretax dollars—sometimes called a cafeteria plan—then the benefits are taxable when received.

So what?

Think of it this way:

Your salary: $60,000 gross income

$48,000 annual budget needed to pay the bills if you cannot work

60 percent disability coverage from your employer = $36,000 (remember it is taxable)

After taxes benefit = $25,200 **(less than 40 percent coverage)**

Supplemental Coverage Needed	=	$48,000	-	$25,200	=	$22,800
	=	Need	-	Benefit	=	Supplemental Coverage Needed

In reality, a 60 percent benefit is really a 40 percent benefit after the IRS gets through with it. What I always ask a person is this: could you handle a 60 percent decrease in salary and still pay the bills? Could you handle a **30 percent** decrease in your take-home pay and still be current on bills?

Also consider this: the insurance company statistics say there is a larger chance of disability than death for the average person.

In some ways disability is worse. When you die your family loses an asset, but if you become disabled, your family loses an asset and you become a liability. Meaning that not only can you not work, but now also someone has to take care of you.

Getting a good disability policy is not as easy as it once was.

The best way is to hire an independent financial adviser who can comparison shop a variety of disability contracts for you. Make sure they are experts in comparing this type of insurance. Similar to buying life insurance, you generally will not pay more for coverage placed by an agent than directly from a company, so use a skilled advisor.

Fake claims and other fraud have spurred the industry to trim the benefits and charge much more for the most desirable provisions.

The decision of what coverage to buy is hard. It is very difficult to compare policies. The policies are also very expensive. Some less expensive policies may not have important benefits that you cannot live without.

Here are some tips to look out for:

The policy should refer to your own occupation. Make sure your policy says that your doctor, not the insurance carrier's doctor or the claims person, decides whether you are disabled.

This is generally not the case for employer-provided group coverage. Take at look at this.

Two possible definitions of disability that must be satisfied to receive benefits:

1. Own Occupation Definition

    "You are disabled if you are unable to perform the duties of your <u>own</u> occupation. Your occupation is defined as what you are doing at the time of disability."

2. Not-An-Own Occupation Definition

    "You are disabled if you cannot perform the duties of <u>any</u> occupation for which you are reasonably trained by education or experience."

You will notice that only one word is different between definitions, but the total meaning is very different. This is why it is so important to have an advisor helping you. You could miss these important differences.

Other benefits to look for are coverage for partial disabilities or partial income loss, defined as lost time or a reduction in pay from your current occupation due to disability. Maybe you can do some work, but if you are still suffering a loss of earning power, you need to be protected. This is generally not a benefit found in employer group coverage.

I could write a whole book on the subject. Consult someone to get help with this one. If you love your family you cannot afford to do without adequate insurance coverage.

In summary, so much detail in this chapter is necessary because insurance seems to be so misunderstood. If it is misunderstood, people end up paying more. This leads to debt and lack of savings.

15

Avoid Debt, Part 5— Reduce Home and Auto Insurance Costs

Along the same lines as evaluating your life insurance for cost effectiveness, you should look at other types of insurance for cutting costs, your home and car insurance in particular. There is great potential for savings here.

First let me go over some background information.

Your home can be insured for:

Replacement Cost—pays you the cost of replacing damaged property with no deduction for depreciation but with a maximum dollar amount.

Guaranteed Replacement Cost—pays the full cost of replacing damaged property with no deduction for depreciation and no dollar limit. Some insurance companies may limit coverage to 120 percent of the cost of rebuilding your home.

Actual Cash Value—pays you an amount equal to the replacement value of damaged property minus a depreciation allowance.

Unless a policy specifically states that property is covered for its replacement value, coverage is usually for actual cash value. Bottom line: Ask your agent. Do not get a surprise at claim time.

I do not profess to be an expert in this area. However, the most common mistake I see a person make is blindly accepting coverage from their agent without asking questions.

People do not realize their agents may not even work on their policies. The commissions are too small. They focus on the bigger fish in the sea (like business insurance).

As a result, an assistant or junior producer may be putting your coverage together. This person may not know your unique situation or needs or even have much experience. Your agent may not even see the coverage or have input. It is not that someone else is not competent, but if you choose to do business with an agent, he or she needs to answer your questions.

Most of the time, when I have received a policy on my home or car, they faxed it to me saying, "Here it is." There was not a lot of dialogue about the coverage or exceptions unless I asked questions. I find many people blindly take the coverage without as so much as asking one question. They waste money this way.

Knowing this, here are some pitfall areas to look for where you should ask questions:

1. What if I am adding on to my home?

If you add improvements to your home, you should increase your coverage. Don't wait until the addition is completed to increase your coverage. Contact your insurance agent before construction begins. Otherwise, if the new addition is damaged or destroyed before you have increased your coverage, you may be responsible for the cost of repairing or rebuilding the addition.

Make sure that contractors and subcontractors working on your addition have workers' compensation and insurance by requesting copies of their insurance certificates. If the coverage is insufficient, you may need to extend the liability limits portion of your homeowner's policy. Workers injured while working on your addition could sue you if the contractor doesn't have the proper insurance coverage.

2. What is a household inventory?

A household inventory is a complete and detailed list of all the personal property located in your dwelling or stored in other structures like garages and tool sheds. Your inventory should include your possessions as well as items owned by individuals who are also insured under your homeowner's policy, such as family members, other household residents, and domestic employees.

Under the terms of your homeowner's policy, your claim for damaged or stolen personal property should show the quantity, description, actual cash value (if different from the purchase price), and amount of loss associated with each item. Copies of bills, receipts, and other documents that justify the figures in your claim are also requested.

Many agents recommend video taping your household inventory in case of a potential loss and eventual claim. You can also pay a third party to do this and make an inventory of you house. Check your phone book under property appraisers.

3. Do I need sewer and drain coverage?

A typical homeowner's policy will not cover damage from water that backs up through sewers or drains or from a sump pump malfunction. Sewer and drain coverage is worthwhile if you have a finished basement with furniture or appliances that may be damaged by water backups.

4. Who is responsible for removing dead trees?

Check with your agent about your responsibility to remove dead trees from your yard. If a tree falls on the neighbor's house, will you be covered?

5. Do I need insurance for jewelry and art?

Homeowners' policies also set specific dollar limits for particular categories of personal property. For some categories, such as jewelry, firearms, and furs, the policy specifies a limit only for theft, not for damage or destruction.

The reason is that these items are especially susceptible to theft, and insurance companies want to limit their exposure to these fairly common incidents. Damage or destruction of these items is less common, and insurance companies are usually willing to cover them up to their actual cash value.

Bottom line—get details on your coverage from your agent.

6. What if I have a home office?

If you are one of a growing number of people working out of your home, you have a special need for business property and business liability insurance protection. Some people can get the extra coverage they need by adding coverage options to their homeowners' insurance policies.

Standard insurance policies also have a maximum payout for stolen or a damaged items and less for items that are stolen outside the home, such as laptops

7. Do I need renter's insurance?

If you live in a condo, town home, tent, or apartment, you need renter's insurance to cover your contents and protect against liability. Ask your agent for help.

8. How to save money on auto insurance

Increase your deductible. For many people, raising the deductible on their auto insurance is a good way to cut the cost of the policy. Sometimes you can reduce your annual premium by 10 percent or more if you increase your deductible from $250 to $500. If you do this, however, make sure you have the financial resources to handle the larger deductible if the time comes.

Narrow the scope of your coverage. If you drive an older car, consider dropping collision and comprehensive coverage. The rationale is that even if the vehicle were severely damaged in an accident, the amount the insurer would pay for repairs or replacement would be relatively small. In some cases, the amount you'd receive might not even cover the costs of the premiums and the deductible.

Take advantage of multiple policy discounts. Most companies offer 10–15 percent discounts if you have home and auto insurance with them.

9. How can I insure my teenager without going broke?

As you have probably discovered, insuring a teenage driver can be very expensive. Drivers under the age of twenty-five pose the greatest risk to insurers because of their high level of at-fault accidents.

Insurance companies seek to limit their exposure by charging higher insurance rates for sixteen- to twenty-four-year-olds than for any other age group.

The least expensive option would probably be to add your teenager to your existing auto insurance policy once he gets his permanent driver's license. Although this can still be an expensive prospect, your teen might be able to take advantage of certain discounts as a driver on your policy (e.g., safe-driver and multiple-car discounts for which you are eligible).

The only way to determine your most cost-effective option is to contact your agent. If you're thinking about purchasing a used car for your teen, be prepared to tell your insurer the makes, models, and years of the cars you're considering. This way, your insurance agent can give you accurate insurance quotes. These quotes can help you decide whether to purchase separate insurance for your son or add him to your policy; they may also help you decide which car to purchase.

Ask your car insurance agent about discounts when:

- your teen is away at college and does not have a car there;

- he/she does have a car at school but is in a state with lower insurance rates than where you live;

- your teen has good grades or has taken driver education classes;

- your car is not driven heavily, has a history of no claims, is equipped with anti-theft systems, and has safety equipment such as air bags;

- Your teen drives an older car—you may be able to drop comprehensive coverage.

10. I lease or have a loan on my car. Do I need special insurance?

Whether you lease your car or have an outstanding auto loan, gap insurance can provide valuable protection during the early years of your car's life.

As we all know, a new car's value drops the minute you drive it off the lot. Unfortunately, if a bus plows into the side of your new car five minutes after you drive it off the lot, your insurance may only cover the actual cash value of the car.

At this point, there's a good chance the insurance pay off isn't enough to pay off your outstanding lease or loan balance.

Gap insurance was created for just such a situation. If a loss occurs (theft, total loss in a collision, etc.), gap insurance will pay the difference between the actual cash value of the vehicle and the current outstanding balance on your loan or lease. You won't get stuck with the difference.

12. What if I use my car for business?

Notify your insurance company if your car is used for business. Business use is excluded from a liability standpoint in most policies. If you have a part-time job or home-based business, ask your agent about this.

13. What is umbrella coverage?

Personal umbrella liability insurance is designed to protect you against a catastrophic lawsuit or judgment. It provides expanded coverage and increases the amount of your liability protection beyond the basic coverage provided under your homeowner's/renter's and auto insurance policies.

Some people mistakenly believe that personal liability insurance is necessary only if they are wealthy or if they are reckless. But accidents can happen anywhere and to anyone. You might hit a bicycle messenger, or a delivery person might slip on your icy porch. No matter how careful you are, you may one day be sued because you injure someone or damage someone's property. Liability insurance protects your assets in the event that this should happen.

Standard homeowners' insurance, renters' insurance, auto insurance, and even some boat insurance policies provide a degree of protection against certain types of personal liability. Personal umbrella liability insurance supplements the basic liability coverage provided by your other insurance—it's designed to kick in when your other liability coverage is tapped out.

Umbrella coverage is available usually from $1 million to $2 million with annual costs of around $150–$400. Get it; we live in a lawsuit-crazy world.

16

Save and Plan for Future Needs—Part 1

Let me start this chapter by getting past some myths regarding savings. The idea of this and the next few chapters is to give you effective ways to save. In other words, how to find the best deal for your buck and maximize your savings.

Some pieces of financial advice sound so right and true that it is hard to believe they are false. Many myths are like the following are false and it is time to put them to rest.

Myth 1: Always keep a six-month cash reserve on hand for emergencies.

You are often better off using cash that is earning less than 5 percent interest to pay credit card debt that is probably costing you more. You can borrow money on your credit card in a pinch. Why waste money on credit card interest just to keep money in a savings account making nothing?

Myth 2: Prepay a mortgage before other debts. Get that house paid off.

Because mortgages typically charge lower interest than credit card debt and interest payments are usually tax deductible, it is wiser to prepay a mortgage only after other debt is paid off.

Myth 3: Pay credit card debt before contributing to an employee 401(k) plan.

If an employer matches any portion of a contribution, this is free money. Contribute enough to get the full match and then pay down debt.

Myth 4: I should invest before paying off debt because I can earn more.

Consider a safe and easy investment. Regardless of which direction the market heads, one of the surest investments you can make is to reduce or eliminate debt.

For example, if you were in the 28 percent marginal tax bracket, you would have to earn a return of 25 percent on a taxable investment for it to be as good as using the money to pay off credit card debt with an 18 percent nondeductible interest rate.

If you are in a higher marginal tax bracket, it is an even better deal.

If you do not have enough deductions to itemize each year and you take the standard deduction, or you are subject to the phase out of itemized deductions because of the high level of your income, it may also make sense to pay down your mortgage by using any excess funds currently invested in certificates of deposits or low-interest money market accounts.

The interest on these types of accounts is taxable, and you are getting little or no benefit from your mortgage interest deductions.

Myth 5: When should I pay off my mortgage? When should I invest?

In our mobile society, most of us do not stay in our homes long enough to pay off a thirty-year mortgage. Even if you can afford to retire your mortgage early, many people believe there are better ways to invest your extra cash.

Still, there is an unquantifiable sense of security that comes from owning your home. In addition, making extra payments on your mortgage will save you thousands of dollars.

There are equally powerful arguments against paying off a mortgage early. Suppose you have a 6.5 percent interest rate on your mortgage. If you deduct mortgage interest from your taxes and you are in the 27 percent tax bracket, the actual rate is closer to 5.1 percent. That means any investment that earns more than 5.1 percent on an after-tax basis will provide a better return on your money.

If you are going to invest rather than pay off a mortgage, invest in something that will give you the opportunity for the best chance to earn returns in excess of the interest paid. One example of an investment could be stock mutual funds.

If you are going to keep the money safe in CDs, pay off your mortgage. You are not getting ahead by investing.

Myth 6: Who will benefit from paying off a mortgage early?

Paying off a mortgage early can benefit some homeowners more than others. Who stands to benefit?

- Homeowners who do not deduct mortgage interest.

  If your mortgage is small, your interest may not even exceed the standard deduction the IRS gives non-itemizing taxpayers. Without the tax break, the actual cost of your mortgage is higher. Paying it off early makes sense.

  Just remember to get an equity line afterward so that you can tap equity in case of an emergency. Talk to your CPA about this one.

- Homeowners who pay Private Mortgage Insurance (PMI)

  Lenders typically charge PMI to borrowers with less than 20 percent equity in their homes. If you are close to 20 percent, making extra payments could put you over the top. Eliminating PMI will reduce your monthly payments, and you will get an immediate return on your investment.

Planning tip—keep track of extra payments on the computer. Write two separate checks: one for the regular payment and one for the prepayment. Clearly make notes in the memo section of your check if you want the money applied to principal.

When you hear someone say that paying off a mortgage loses tax advantage, realize this is someone who knows nothing about your situation unless they are your CPA.

Think about how taxes work. For every $1 that is deductible, you get back around 3¢–4¢. But you still paid 7¢. What if I said to you for every dollar you give me, I will give you back seventy cents. Not a bad deal? That is taxes.

Anyone making those statements about losing tax advantage generally does not know what he or she is talking about.

That goes for first-time homebuyers as well, who think they are losing because they do not own a home. The interest deduction only benefits someone above the level of the standard deduction. Get help from your CPA.

17

Saving & Planning— A Biblical Approach to Investments

I am always amazed at how people arrive at decisions on where and how to invest their money. This seems to be an area in which people often listen too much to the opinions of others.

I do not want to bore you with a history lesson of information that you already know, but people seem to need a reminder of the facts. So much of this is common sense—not opinions, but facts.

What does history tell us? What does the Bible tell us? Are there basic principles in history and in the Bible to guide us in our decision making regarding investments?

You bet!

At the time of the writing of this book, the economy has just come through 9/11 and the biggest stock market loss since the Great Depression. What did we learn?

People have been coming into my office for the past few years thinking that the world was coming to an end. Sure it has been a tough time, but is it really unique to history? Is this a unique investment time?

There are three keys to choosing investments and an investment strategy:

Principle 1: Understand historical performance to remove emotions.

Fact—the stock market rewards patience.

Many investors make mistakes during falling markets, such as we have experienced in recent years. It is easy to lose perspective and panic by listening to the negative comments of television moderators and newspaper columnists. Those who ignore history are doomed to repeat it.

Many people make decisions based on the opinions of others rather than going to the library and getting the facts.

Many investors have no plan and invest by the seat of their pants. They are easily influenced by the opinions of others and get off track. If the investor had a plan, the probability is he or she should stay with it.

The market will have its ups and downs: You must be patient and take a long-term view. The following table shows how much Standard & Poor's 500 Index fell during the eight most recent down markets and how many months it took to recoup the loss.

This table goes directly to the fear that we are in a unique investment time.

Down Market Period	Drop in S&P 500 Index	Months of Decline	Months to Break Even
Dec. 1961–June 1962	-28.00%	6.50	21.00
Feb. 1966–Oct. 1966	-22.20	7.90	15.00
Nov. 1968–May 1970	-36.10	17.90	39.80
Jan. 1973–Oct. 1974	-48.20	20.70	91.50
Sept. 1976–Mar. 1978	-19.40	17.20	35.30
Nov. 1980–Aug. 1982	-27.10	20.50	23.50
Aug. 1987–Dec. 1987	-33.50	3.20	23.40
July 1990–Dec. 1990	-19.90	2.80	7.10
Average	-29.30	12.10	32.10

What does this tell you?

Look how bad some of these periods were. In 1962 we had the Cuban Missile Crisis. In 1963 Kennedy was assassinated. In 1987 was Black Monday, and in 1990 we had the Gulf War.

No matter how bad it was during these times, the market always came back in time. The real question is how long did it take to recover? If you were not patient and sold your stock during these "bad" times, then you missed the eventual recovery.

I wish I had a dollar for every time I have heard in recent years:

- "This market is different."

- "We are at war with Iraq."

- "Preventing terrorism will cost the economy trillions."

- "Tax cuts are only for the rich."

- "Gas prices are too high."

- The Democrats are going to be the end of the market

I know this a little ridiculous, but people need to be reminded of the past and that history proves things will get better. Stay focused, and be patient. Do not invest with your emotions.

Principle 2: Avoid market timing by staying focused and staying invested.

Some investors like to wait for just the right moment to get into the stock market and for just the right time to pull their investments out.

If that sounds like you, there is something you should know. While you are sitting on the sidelines, some of the market's best single-day performances could slip right past you. Are you so confident in your timing strategy that you are willing to forfeit those gains?

Missing even a handful of the market's best days could cost you dearly. If you had invested $10,000 in the S&P 500 on December 31, 1995, by December 31, 2000, your $10,000 would have grown to $23,196, an average annual total return of 18.33 percent.

Suppose during that five-year period there were times when you decided to get out of the market and, as a result, you missed the market's ten best single-day performances. In that case, your 18.33 percent return would have fallen to 9.24 percent.

If you had missed the market's twenty best days, the 18.33 percent return would have dropped to 2.98 percent.

While past performance cannot guarantee comparable future results, it provides us insight into the difficulty of market timing. Can you do it successfully every time?

Even the best stock pickers out there miss once in a while. Is it really worth it? If they cannot do it, can you?

That is why smart investors do not play the timing game. They do not let the market's short-term gyrations sideline them or dictate their investment objectives.

They are patient investors—focused on the long term and their long-term goals.

Consider this table:

The Penalty for Missing the Market		
Trying to time the market can be an inexact—and costly—exercise. S&P 500 Index: December 31, 1995–December 31, 2000		
PERIOD OF INVESTMENT	AVERAGE ANNUAL TOTAL RETURN	GROWTH OF $10,000
Fully Invested	18.33%	$23,196
Miss the 10 Best Days	9.24%	$15,557
Miss the 20 Best Days	2.98%	$11,583
Miss the 30 Best Days	-2.07%	$9,006
Miss the 40 Best Days	-6.38%	$7,191
Miss the 60 Best Days	-13.70%	$4,787

Sources: Standard & Poor's; Bloomberg Calculations by AIM Distributors, Inc.

What is with the need to time the market?

I have never met anyone that can do this consistently. To me, it is like driving a car through rush hour traffic.

Have you ever noticed that some people weave through traffic, trying to get to their destinations faster, only to be caught at the next light? What did it accomplish? Why take the risk of wrecking? People like this live short lives because they take too many risks, and the stress of living gets them eventually.

Here is another analogy: Suppose you play tennis. You are standing at the net, and your opponent hits a lob. You have to make a split-second decision of whether or not to keep the ball in play or smash it for an outright winner.

Before making the decision, suppose you knew the following: If you just kept the ball in play, you would win the point every time. If you smash the ball for an outright winner, there is a 30 percent chance you would hit the ball into the net. Which would you choose?

Principle 3: Determine income and liquidity needs.

Define how much income you need from your investments. If you need $2,000 monthly and you can get 8 percent from a fixed-income investment, then you need to invest $300,000 to generate $2,000 of monthly income.

If you do not have that much capital, you will need to use some of your principal each month to meet your needs. You may have to reduce your income needs or take more risk by investing in stocks and hoping the return over time is sufficient and consistent to generate your income needs. Once the income needs are met, allocate the remainder toward growth while maintaining sufficient liquidity.

The major point here is that the stock market is for long-term goals.

You must keep three to six months of liquidity outside or, at a minimum, have access to an equity line. If your time frame for needing the money is less than 5 years, you should not even invest in the stock market.

Instead, people invest in the stock market for a short-term goal and then wonder what to do when the market corrects (declines) right before they need the money.

I am reminded of a client that came in to see me with a big problem. He had been investing on his own in technology stocks for his kid's college costs. He would need money in about nine months. The market corrected, and he lost half of his savings on paper. He did not have time for the market to come back.

What could he have done? Was investing in technology stocks a bad idea? This approach had paid off in recent months, but what now?

The reality is that he should have been shifting money to safe investments a long time ago; he was 100 percent invested in stocks! Greed caused him to take too much risk. It would now take years to recoup lost principal. It is tough to sell investments doubling in value every six months like technology stock were at the time.

This sets up principle 4. He did not have a plan. He did not match the risk levels with the needed liquidity.

Principle 4: Understand asset allocation.

This is the most important step and the one that is supported the most in the Bible. Asset allocation is clearly a biblical principle. I figure if God said do it, it must be important.

Choosing your investments is one of the most confusing and potentially costly decisions you will ever make. Finding the right mix of growth and income is difficult to do. Not every investor has the same tolerance for risk or the same needs for current income and liquidity for emergencies. What seems risky to one investor may be conservative to another. Stop listening to how others invest.

An asset allocation plan will help you determine if you have the right mix of investments for your personal situation. Development of a personalized asset allocation plan provides a disciplined and systematic approach to investing. It guides you from defining your personal investment objectives to determining a suitable portfolio.

With all of the investment choices available today from banks, brokerage companies, and insurance companies, you need help to evaluate the many choices and create a well-designed plan specific to your needs.

The purpose of an asset allocation plan is to determine how your investment assets should be divided among the available investment alternatives. Your plan will usually depend on your financial objectives, time horizon, risk tolerance, and present financial situation.

Studies show that your asset allocation plan can determine over 90 percent of the performance of your investment portfolio.

How you allocate your investment dollars far outweighs the potential effects of your stock selection and market timing.

Asset allocation is based on the Nobel—Prize-winning concept of the modern portfolio theory.

Through intelligent diversification you can protect against many investment risks. Gains in one investment may help offset losses in another.

Asset allocation involves spreading your assets across a variety of sectors, regions, market caps, and economies, and in a range of investment vehicles. Because you maintain broadly diversified portfolios such as those offered through many mutual funds, you know that when one asset class or investment vehicle experiences losses, others may experience gains

How important is asset allocation? Consider that it's biblical.

Ecclesiastes 11:2

"Give portions to seven, yes to eight, for you do not know what disaster may come upon the land."

So what exactly does it mean?

There are a number of asset classes that have investment merit. We know they have investment merit because each class has a long history of returns showing its behavior.

By class, I mean a category of similar investments such as large growth stocks, real estate, etc.

If you look at the history of each asset class, you will notice that different asset classes will outperform other asset classes during varying economic periods.

For example, international stocks were the best performing class of stocks in 1986, 1987, and 1993. If you had all your money invested in that class, you would have made the most money those years.

In 1989, 1992, 1995, and 1997, international stocks were the worst class you could have invested in. If you had all your money invested in that class, you would have lost the most money those years.

Most of the money being made in the stock market comes from being in the right asset class at the right time. As market conditions change, asset classes become more or less favorable.

The bottom line with asset allocation is that you are not guessing which asset classes will perform best or worst in the future, but instead blending the right mix to achieve a consistent return according to your risk tolerance.

Asset allocation takes advantage of the fact that different asset classes perform better than others during varying economic periods. By blending the right mix of assets, you reduce your risk and achieve a more consistent return.

Example of an Asset Allocation Plan

Proposed Asset Allocation

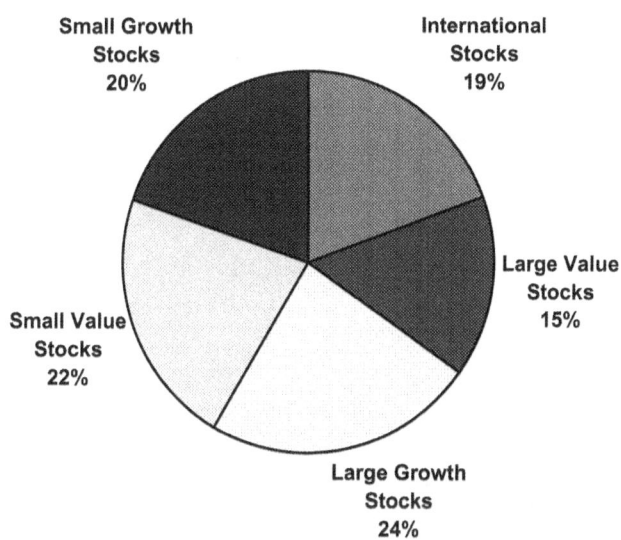

Small Growth Stocks 20%

International Stocks 19%

Large Value Stocks 15%

Small Value Stocks 22%

Large Growth Stocks 24%

Range of Returns

The range of average annual returns for the proposed asset mix is:

1 Year Period	5 Years	10 Years	20 Years
48.0% to -21.3%	25.9% to -2.9%	21.5% to 3.6%	18.5% to 4.9%

Simulated range of returns means the most likely future returns over some given period of time. In other words, the above investment example held for twenty years would yield a return of 18 percent with a worst-case scenario of 4 percent.

The range of average narrows over longer time periods and for more conservative portfolios.

These returns are based on past performance. While past performance is no guarantee of the future, it is, in my opinion the best indicator of the future. History does repeat itself.

This would be a good mix for retirement savings if you were young. Being young, you can afford to ignore short term market corrections. This would not be a good mix if you were sixty and retiring in a few years.

To contrast the mix, suppose you could have an allocation as follows:

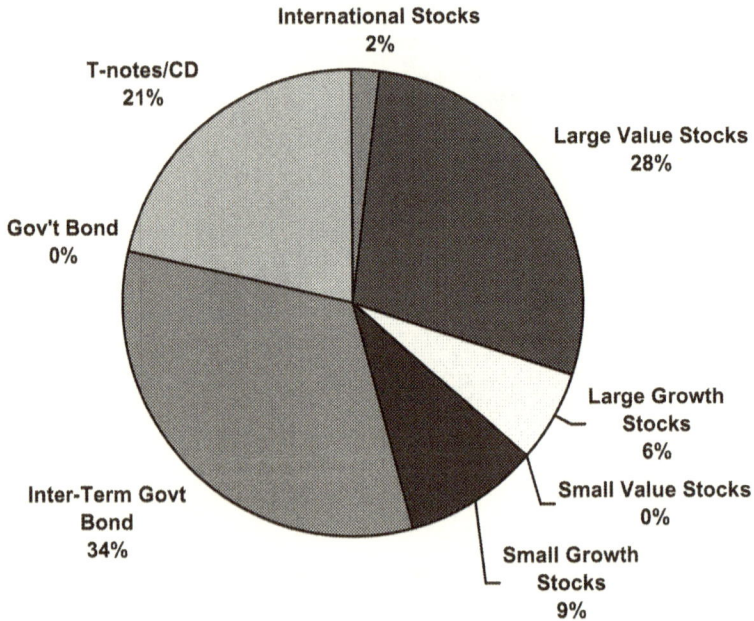

If we look back in recent years, a portfolio like the above example would have lost 1–5 percent. That is pretty amazing considering, at the time of the book's writing, the previous few years was during the biggest market crash since the depression (months after 9/11), and over a twenty-year period would have averaged around 3–8 percent.

Not a bad trade-off of risk and return.

You will notice the "pie" looks different from the previous example. Mainly, the money is invested in more safe investments like bonds. The two examples contrast returns and risks.

The point to illustrate is that everyone should have his or her own plan that is guided by a savings goal.

So how can you do this for yourself? Check out two Web sites: www.money.com and www.riskgrades.com. You will find great information on how to design the right allocation plan for you depending on your time horizon, risk tolerance, and many other important factors. Read the questions asked carefully.

While there are numerous discussions regarding non-loaded versus loaded funds and index funds, both sides have good arguments. The big deal for me is not whether you avoid sales commissions when investing money. As a financial advisor, I realize I am a little biased.

I would agree with people—if they can invest by themselves, by all means do it. Why pay fees if you do not need or want the help?

But for the rest of people who want help or are unsure about investing, I would rather they pay for help than screw it up on their own just because *Money* magazine says to invest in some fund. You cannot, in my opinion, get personalized investment help without seeing someone. Certainly not from a magazine or CNBC.

Some people do not like CPAs giving investment advice. I disagree—my CPA is smarter than me. He gives me advice and I know more about finances than most

The key question is: can you do this yourself without help?

My biggest issue is with professionals not emphasizing asset allocation. Many brokers focus on hot stocks and ignore the merits of modern portfolio theory. If that is the case, fire them. They should spend most of their time on customizing an asset allocation plan for you and not hot stock tips.

If they are not, get rid of them.

Furthermore, while I like *Money* magazine, it is no substitute for much-needed professional advice. A good advisor or CPA should add value well in excess of what they charge for the advice.

18

Finding Specific Investments to Fulfill Your Asset Allocation Plan

The outcome of an asset allocation plan is determining an investment mix that provides the most efficient portfolio that measures the best trade-off of risk and return. Once a plan is known, you choose specific investments to fulfill it. Please be advised that mutual fund investing involves risk, including the potential for principal loss.

Since most people use mutual funds, this chapter is devoted to selecting good funds.

Steps to choosing investment products to fulfill an asset allocation plan:

Step 1: Evaluate a fund's correlation to style.

In selecting different assets or mutual funds to fulfill an asset allocation plan, it is important to determine how well a mutual fund stock follows a stated asset class style, such as a large company value. Independent technical information firms, such as Morningstar and Value Line, provide this information.

Here are their Web sites: www.morningstar.com and www.valueline.com.

Independent information is essential to determine the type of mutual funds to own. You cannot just look at returns. A certain type of funds may have been out of favor in recent years. The return may look bad even though it is a great fund.

Furthermore, many companies use misleading names that do not truly describe the holdings. The key is that you only want to look at funds that are consistent with the asset class they represent. The evaluated returns should be from a stated asset class, not from mutual funds across the board.

Step 2: Evaluate performance relative to peer group.

Use the cumulative annual performance to compare how well a fund performs relative to its peer group, not funds in general. Again, funds can underperform in the market for a period of time but still be good funds to invest in.

The bottom line—over a long period of time, look at how well a mutual fund manager has performed; performance should be relative to other funds in its class. The time period should be at a minimum ten years to give a good picture of how well a fund performs over a complete market cycle.

Using the above Web sites, you can search for a certain category and pick the best funds in each category. What to look for are funds that have high "star "ratings over a ten year period. See Web sites for further explanation.

If you do not want to subscribe to these sites, you can find the information at the library.

Step 3: Evaluate a minimum track record.

When selecting mutual funds, it is critical to evaluate performance over a long period of time (at least ten years with the same manager). During that period, how well has a fund performed? Has it been a consistent top performer with a high star rating?

By eliminating funds that do not have a ten-year track record with the same manager, you throw out a lot of good funds, but it gives you a meaningful record to evaluate. It could be that new fund manger will move to top of performer in time, but I would rather wait and see if that happens before investing.

Step 4: Expense Ratio (cost of expenses in fund)

How well does the manager control expenses and maximize return? Do you have to pay sales loads? Can you find a non-loaded alternative? Morningstar provides this information on funds.

Step 5: Conduct a periodic review and make changes if needed.

How well has the fund performed in relationship to its peer class? Have there been manager changes or fund style changes? Has your asset allocation plan changed? You must continue to review your mix based on asset performance and life changes.

The percentage weighting to each asset class within the investment portfolio will vary. The percentage weighting within each asset class will be allowed to vary within a reasonable range of +/- 5–10 percent, depending on market conditions.

The single biggest mistake I see people make with investments is that they do not rebalance their portfolio periodically.

What does rebalancing mean?

Here is an example; suppose your plan looks like this:

25 percent large company growth

25 percent large company value

25 percent small company growth

25 percent international stocks

One certainty is that after some time, six months to one year, this allocation will be different, primarily because some asset classes make money during that period and some do not.

Suppose the following happened:

40 percent large company growth	Made 15 percent during the period
25 percent large company value	No gain
25 percent small company growth	No Gain
10 percent international stocks	Lost 15 percent during the period

So what should you do?

The answer is sell some of the large company growth stock funds and buy international stocks.

This brings the original allocation back in balance. This is needed because the two asset classes are no longer 25 percent of the total money. Large company stock is greater than 25 percent and international stock is less than 25 percent.

This is called rebalancing. It is crucial to keeping risk constant. Without rebalancing, you would have too much of your money in large company stock.

What happens if large company stocks have a bad year?

We know from history that leadership rotates between asset classes. What is on top today will eventually be on bottom in years to come. Nothing will be a winner year in and year out. If you do not rebalance periodically, you may eventually lose all the benefits of diversification.

This is why it is such a common mistake. Many people are able to design good allocations, but they never look at them again. Is this not what happened to those investors who lost everything when Internet stocks plunged in the early 2000s?

What seemed to happen is that people only devoted a small portion of their investment portfolios to Internet and technology stocks. They may have known that these types of stocks are risky.

But Internet stocks made so much money quickly. What started out as 5 percent of someone's portfolio quickly became 50 percent. People never sold their gains and reinvested into asset classes that were having a down year.

Without rebalancing, people lost a lot of their portfolio when Internet stocks plunged.

The reason this works is that it forces us to invest without emotions. It is not a natural thing to sell stocks doing well and buy ones not doing so well. The asset allocation plan forces us to stick with the original plan that in the long run meets our needs.

19

Saving and Planning for the Dreaded College Costs

Outside of retirement and the purchase of a home, paying for a college education for our children is likely the biggest, most expensive savings goal we will face in our lifetimes.

Bearing the cost of a child's education may feel like paying off the national debt. Financing a college education requires planning and foresight. However, it could be the single most important investment in an individual's life. An investment in higher education usually doubles or triples lifetime earning power.

Recent tax legislation created several opportunities for parents saving for college. However, there is a lot of confusion regarding different plans. For example, education savings accounts were created for parents, grandparents, and others to make annual contributions to a child's educational fund. Contributions are made into a tax-deferred account with after-tax dollars. Proceeds may be withdrawn tax free for college.

Are education savings plans the best plan? Before considering this, people need to be reminded of the most important variable in saving-time.

IMPORTANCE OF STARTING SAVINGS GOALS EARLY

Desired savings at college	$8000
Rate of return	8 percent

What amount of principal is needed to accumulate $8000 for college without tax considerations?

Time	Amount Saved	Total Amount Saved	Value at Age 18
Invest (birth)	$2000	$2000	$8000
Wait 5 years	$29.93/month Until age 18	$4669	$8000
Wait 10 years	$60.49/month Until age 18	$4807	$8000

As you can see, if you wait just a few years to begin savings, you must contribute over 50 percent more principal to yield the same $8000 for college. *A little savings over a long period of time is better than a large amount of savings over a little period of time.*

I know it is easy to procrastinate with long-term goals. This is why I get so angry at parents about saving for college. They need to start with something—anything—when the baby is born. Most parents wait, thinking they can deal with it later. Big mistake; they run out of time.

In the past, many parents saved by setting up an account for college in the child's name. The primary purpose was to save on taxes. Grandparents often did this so that the money would definitely go to the grandchild.

Any existing savings account in a child's name should be reviewed to determine advantages and its effects on the financial-aid laws. Most parents will find this type of account can hurt more than it helps. The new savings opportunities create many alternatives to saving in your child's name but not through traditional custodial accounts.

A relatively new option is to invest in the Prepaid Affordable College Tuition (PACT) plan. This state-sponsored plan allows parents to prepay the cost of tuition and fees for college at today's costs. This is a very attractive option with some limitations for private or out-of-state schools. By locking into college costs today, your rate of return is the inflation rate of college, which has been high in recent years.

So how do you choose? Where should you save to get the best bang for your buck?

Here are some general guidelines I give to clients:

—If you will be the age fifty-nine and one-half (IRS retirement age) or older when money is needed for college, you should use your 401(k), IRA, or some other pre-tax contribution vehicle, especially if there is an employer match.

While the proceeds are taxable when used versus other plans, pretax money together with matches, in my opinion, outweigh this over the long run. The key to why this works is taking deductions on contributions and avoiding normal withdrawal penalties. My experience is that you will wind up with more money in the end because of compound interest. You will have more money working for you, over a longer time, because you did not pay taxes on the contribution. Otherwise for every dollar saved, you would actually have to save $1.20-$1.50 before taxes.

Older parents have the opportunity to save pretax for college. This is a huge benefit. This, together with the fact that it does not usually affect financial-aid eligibility, makes it a winner. Currently retirement plans are excluded assets from financial aid eligibility.

Unfortunately this idea will not apply to most parents unless they have children in your forties.

—If you will be around fifty-three years old when withdrawals are needed for college, you can still use your 401(k), IRA, and other pretax vehicles to save. To avoid a penalty at age fifty-nine and a half, fund college expenses with student loans and pay off the loans after age fifty-nine and a half with your retirement savings.

Remember, if you try to use retirement money before you're fifty-nine and a half years old, the IRS will penalize you.

The key to remember about saving for college is, regardless of their success in saving, paying for 100 percent of your child's college is out of reach. Most people just cannot do it. However, this does not take parents off the hook. They need to make every effort possible to save and minimize frivolous spending on cars and other materialistic things.

If you are not saving money by the time your kids are born, you are behind. It is possible for every parent to save $50–$100 a month from the time of a child's birth. However, parents do not discipline themselves enough, or feel a sense of urgency about saving. You just have to start saving no to other things.

—If you will have a strong need for financial aid when your kids are in school, you should consider choosing investments owned by you and in your name. You might even consider allowing the investments to be owned by a grandparent to gain tax advantages and maximize financial aid.

Have grandparents gift the tuition directly to the school when needed from their savings. This idea assumes that they write the tuition check directly to college and that they are financially secure—free of Medicaid worries. If there are Medicaid or nursing home worries, this is not a good idea.

—If you have a moderate need for financial aid, your primary choice should be to utilize an educational IRA. However, there are income requirements that restrict many people from contributing. If you are not eligible, you should probably use a 529 plan.

—If you have very little tolerance for investment risk, you should consider savings bonds or the PACT plan.

Many times people ask me if they can convert a custodial account for a child to a 529 plan. The answer is yes, with many catches. Often those types of accounts were set up before the existence of new alternatives.

The new tax law has made investment programs such as the 529 plan much more attractive than custodial accounts. Withdrawals will be fully tax-free if they are used for college. This means that no taxes need to be paid at any time during the life of these plans.

Custodial accounts for children are at a severe tax disadvantage. Taxes may be due on the income each year, and the gain on the account's assets is taxable to beneficiaries when those investments are subsequently sold.

Rollovers are allowed, but there are some traps for the unwary: To do a transfer from a custodial account to a 529 plan, you must first sell the assets in the custodial account, and taxes must be paid on any gain. Amounts rolled over retain their status as custodial assets, and the child has control of the account at the age of majority.

If you need additional information on 529 plans, try www.savingforcollege.com. This is a great Web site.

Once your children are in college, there are several techniques to save money. These ideas will help you minimize student-loan debt:

1. Have overdraft protection placed on their checking accounts. Bounced checks are common for students. Have the credit overdraft statements duplicated and mailed to your home as well as the students' homes.

2. Install the Quicken program on their computers to help them learn to keep records of expenses. Teach them that credit cards are like drugs with quick pleasure and long-term pain. If they learn that credit cards only give the illusion of having more money, they will be way ahead in their adult lives. Follow the $100 rule. Encourage your children to consult you before buying anything that costs more than $100.

3. Teach students to avoid purchasing prepackaged convenience items and to purchase frequently used items in bulk. Investigate college-based cafeteria plans.

4. Consider purchasing a condo or mobile home and substitute mortgage payments for nondeductible rent payments. As long as you set reasonable rent, you can write off the interest, taxes, condo fees, repairs, and depreciation. You can even possibly pay a salary to your children as resident managers. Check with your CPA for details. Sell the asset after college to recoup your expenses. Success in this area alone may pay for college. Consult your CPA if necessary.

5. Send your college students off with a credit card that is in your name with the students as cosigners. You will be able to see monthly statements and monitor spending.

6. Use tuition payment plans; they allow you to pay tuition in installments for budgeting purposes. Most plans have no finance charges, just enrollment fees. You can find Academic Management Services, Knight Resource Group, or Tuition Management Systems on the Internet for details.

7. Ask your insurance company about discounts for cars that are kept at home if the students' colleges are more than one hundred miles away.

20

Saving for College, Continued

Because financial aid is such a big part of sending your kids to college, you need to know the rules. Knowing these rules will allow you to maximize the success of your college planning.

A reality for most parents is that they will need some type of assistance. This is a discouraging fact. Most parents could do a lot better saving for college; however, it would require some serious spending changes that I know many parents won't make. Therefore, when considering college plans you have to consider financial-aid eligibility.

The beginning point is to understanding financial need. What is financial need? Many parents do not want to talk about or learn about financial aid because they think they will never qualify.

Financial Need = Cost of Attendance - Expected Family Contribution

The college sets the cost of attendance. This includes tuition, fees, and allowances for needs such as room, board, and other expenses. It differs for each school.

The family contribution is the annual amount the government expects you to contribute toward the cost of education. This number is determined when you complete the financial aid (Free Application for Federal Student Aid or FAFSA) process. The family contribution is the same regardless of which college you attend and is based on income and assets.

Here is how the process works, step by step:

Step 1: Call all schools your child is interested in and request the entire financial-aid package.

This is crucial because some universities have their own form or will require a Financial Aid Application (FAF). Form FAF is in addition to the FAFSA (required government form). Make sure you are sent all deadlines for paperwork to be submitted.

Step 2: Complete FAFSA one time, online.

Earliest filing date is January 1 of the student's senior year of high school. Deadline is May 1 of the year in which aid is sought. The application is free and automatically applies for federal, most state, and some campus-based programs. If tax returns are not completed by filing deadlines, estimates are allowed. Send application certified mail or complete online at the Department of Education's Web site.

Step 3: Complete FAF if required by the school of interest.

FAF may be required in addition to the FAFSA. The FAF is not free. For each college that you are interested in, there is a charge for sending the results to them. Some colleges may not require it.

Step 4: Receive the Student Aid Report (SAR).

Your application with the Department of Education should be processed in four weeks. The SAR is the end result. You will receive a report with your expected family contribution. The same report is sent to the state's higher education agency of any designated colleges.

The college you apply to may verify you through an audit. What an IRS audit means to taxpayers, verification means to financial-aid applicants. It means someone wants to see the records that support the numbers on your form. The government's computers randomly select about one-third of all applications for verification. If you are selected, your SAR will inform you near the bottom of page 1.

Step 5: Correct SAR if necessary.

A computer processes the SAR. If you have omitted information or an error was made, this is the time for correction. If the SAR is correct, send a copy of the report and letter directly to the financial-aid office requesting a meeting with the financial-aid office. Your designated schools will receive the information directly; however, this personalizes your application and sets up a meeting.

Step 6: Complete additional applications for institutional/state aid if necessary.

Specific states and universities may require additional forms. The financial-aid office may also require additional information on parents/stepparents, balance sheets/income projections for business owners, and verification of information through tax returns and other information.

Step 7: Meet with financial-aid office.

This will outline the financial-aid package for each specific university. You may accept or reject the offer. This is your opportunity to negotiate a better package.

Most of the processing up to this point has been impersonal through computers. If you want your situation to be looked at closely, you must call attention to it. Now is the time to plead your case. You should describe your situation in the letter and follow it up with a meeting. Financial-aid offices will consider better packages for special circumstances (loss of job, divorce, etc.).

Step 8: Follow up with bursar's office in August to make sure all of the grants/loans have been credited to your tuition bill.

Step 9: Complete renewal applications.

Annually, a new application must be completed and the process repeats itself.

The reason I am going into this much detail on the process is so that I can set up an understanding of the most common mistake parents make. If parents will need aid to send their kids to college, they need to understand where they can go wrong.

In past years, colleges provided financial aid on an informal and personal basis. In 1992, because of an increased demand and cost for higher education, the government mandated the use of a single methodology.

These guidelines are now used to determine eligibility for federally funded student aid programs.

Qualifying for financial aid is even tougher than getting a deduction from the IRS. In order for parents to successfully navigate the process, they must first understand what not to do. Here is a summary of the biggest mistakes parents make:

Mistake 1: Assuming you are not eligible for financial aid.

Seventy percent of aid comes from the federal government. Unfortunately, many parents believe incorrectly that they must be on welfare to qualify. Aid is available to students who demonstrate "financial need."

Families show need when the cost of education is greater than their expected contribution. The expected contribution is the amount the government expects you to be able to contribute toward college (remember the formula). It is based on your assets and income and will be the same for any college. Because of the increased cost of college, many people will find that they have need.

Financial Need = Cost of Education - Expected Contribution

Bottom line—limiting school choice to reduce tuition costs does not necessarily reduce a parent's share of college expense. The higher the school cost, the higher the need.

Mistake 2: Assuming an in-state school will cost less than an out-of-state or private school.

Conventional wisdom tells you that state colleges are less expensive than out-of-state or private schools.

Because your expected contribution is the same for every school, the higher the cost of education, the greater the financial need.

Colleges may supplement federal programs with endowments and other sources of aid. A board of trustees controls private colleges while state schools have guidelines set by the government. Private schools have more flexibility to distribute funds and usually have wealthier endowments than state schools.

Therefore, you may have a better chance of having more of your "financial need" filled by a private school than a state school. A higher cost of education does not necessarily mean you pay more.

Limiting school choice to reduce tuition costs does not necessarily reduce a parent's share of college expense. The higher the school cost, the higher the need. Mistakes 1 and 2 are essentially the same.

Mistake 3: Assuming your child will get a scholarship.

Many people believe merit-based and special-situation scholarships are the answers to their prayers. In reality, 80 percent of aid awarded to students comes from the federal and state programs, another 19 percent from institutional and other sources, and only 1 percent from scholarships.

Not only are scholarships difficult to find, they will not reduce the amount of the money you spend for your child's education. A scholarship will reduce the tuition bill, but it will not reduce your share of the bill. Scholarships usually are a dollar for dollar reduction of "financial need," thus reducing the amount of aid you may receive.

Focus your time first on the federal, state, and institutional aid, not scholarship searches. Once the process is completed, look for scholarships to supplement aid and minimize loans.

Mistake 4: Thinking the extra money your child will earn for school will reduce your share of the bill.

Did you know your child would be penalized for taking financial responsibility for part of the cost of school?

Since many parents will need their children to share in the cost of an education, it is crucial that you understand how your child's income affects eligibility for aid. Income the child earns actually counts against him or her, thus reducing aid.

If you would like your child to work, you must understand the value of work-study and cooperative education programs. These programs do not affect aid; check them out at the financial-aid office.

Mistake 5: Improperly using existing college savings and gifts from grandparents.

Many parents have saved money for college or received gifts from their children's grandparents. If you don't know when and how to use these funds, you may give away financial aid for which you are eligible. Many times savings are accumulated in a student's name for tax benefits. This is a huge financial-aid disaster if proper planning is not done. Assets saved in the child's name or gifted directly to the student really hurt chances for aid.

Tip: Obtain loans and have the grandparents repay the loan during the payback period. See mistake 9 for further explanation.

Mistake 6: Not being open-minded to student loans.

Many people refuse to borrow to supplement savings and financial grants. This is a mistake. Most school loans have low interest rates and many allow deferment of interest and principal repayment until graduation.

If you are in the 28 percent tax bracket and do not apply for aid, you must earn $1.39 to have $1.00 to use for tuition. In other words, $1.00 of aid is worth $1.39 to you.

If you project the cost of borrowing until graduation, you may be better off keeping your savings, borrowing the money, and then using your savings to repay the loan. Talk to your CPA or advisor.

Mistake 7: Waiting to start the process.

Many financial-aid programs and scholarships are provided on a first come, first served basis. Schools have different deadlines and applications. Even if your child does not know where he or she would like to attend college, you must start planning now in order to maximize aid. Financial-aid offices are understaffed and overworked. You must apply early.

Tip: Aid decisions are based on your financial situation during your child's junior year in high school. Planning early is crucial to the process. All financial decisions from January 1 of a child's junior year to December 31 of a child's senior year could help or hurt his or her chances of receiving aid.

People who are uninformed about financial aid or wait too long to start the process often get scared and make planning mistakes.

For example, some families will spend their savings on college tuition—money they really need for their own retirement. Others will borrow money at unnecessarily high interest rates or sell their investments at the wrong time, resulting in penalties.

Still others will spend all their energy looking for special scholarships in the false hope that a scholarship will ease the tuition burden, or they will ask their child to consider colleges that are not right for him or her because they think they will save themselves some money.

Finally, the truly uninformed will apply for aid incorrectly so the money runs out before they get their full share or, even worse, neglect to file for financial aid at all because they assume they are not going to qualify.

Mistake 8: Accepting financial-aid packages without negotiating.

Situations that require financial-aid office negotiations are: divorce, illness, student income to support the family, lost job, an unusually good year income wise, social security payments to children that end, uncollected alimony, unanticipated medical expenses, high secondary tuition, among others. These should be discussed with the financial-aid office.

Remember the process is very computerized. You must bring special situations to life with the financial-aid office. The office has the power to give your child a better aid package.

Mistake 9: Selling college savings at the wrong time

This is a frequent mistake. When you sell appreciated assets for college during January of your child's junior year, or after, assets sold are considered annual income even though the asset is sold once. The more income or assets a child or parent has, the less the amount of aid.

The key is to avoid financial transactions between January of your child's junior year and December of his or her senior year.

If your child is already in this crucial period of high school, consider borrowing against countable assets instead of selling them and using college savings to pay back loans when the education is completed.

21

More Money-Saving Ideas

Along the lines of making smart investment decisions for retirement or college are a couple of good ideas for things to do that will save you a lot of money.

Idea 1: Know what's in your credit report.

With the age of fraud and identity theft, you should order your credit reports annually. The main reason for this is to obtain credit scores. Once you know your score, you can begin to understand how it affects your life and work to improve it.

Many people do not understand them, but in reality, credit scores are here to stay. Many lenders feel scores give a good indication of risk. Scores affect your rate. The better your credit score, the better the loan rate.

Credit scoring has also made its way to auto and home insurance. Your credit score now influences your premiums. If your score is not good, you may not even get insurance.

I have been told that even employers are now looking at scores before hiring people. It could be true that your next job hire could be affected.

Overall, credit scores are here to stay. Many people feel that gives a good indication of risk. This is definitely true in the mortgage business. Banks have studied mortgages for years and are convinced that credit scores steers them away from a bad loan.

The best way to improve your score is to obtain and make sure your report is accurate. A record that reflects on-time payments is the goal. Check with all three credit-reporting bureaus, because you may find errors on one report that are not on the others:

Equifax	www.equifax.com
Experian	www.experian.com
TransUnion	www.transunion.com

Even better, recent legislation allows everyone to get his or her report free once a year. In the past, you had to pay twenty-five dollars or more. Remember, it is important that you request all three bureaus since they do not all have the same information.

Once you have your report, here is what to do:

1. Review for correct information. If you find any errors, complete the dispute paperwork and send it back. Do not call the companies that issued the credit. Go directly to the source—the credit bureau.

2. Look for open, inactive accounts. Just because you do not use that old Macy's account does not mean it is closed. You must write or call individually to each credit account to request that it be closed. This may not help your scores immensely, but it will cut down on credit fraud.

    Be sure to request that the credit issuer send a letter stating the account is closed. You will need to follow up repeatedly until everyone complies with the request.

3. Ask to be deleted from mailing lists. A recent law requires credit issuers to allow you to be removed from direct mailing lists. This not only cuts down on junk mail but also prevents "preapproved" applications from falling into the wrong hands. Request this when contacting the credit bureau.

4. Put a fraud alert on your account. Check the credit reporting agencies web sites for details.

Idea 2: Know what kind of improvements increase your home's value.

Another area that requires discussion is improving your home. Many people mistakenly believe they are making money on every improvement to the house. Unfortunately, when sale time comes, they find out that most of the time, they do not even get their money back.

People often confuse necessary home maintenance with improvements. Check out the following:

How Not to Make Money in Real Estate

Not a do-it-yourselfer? Here is how much of your costs you will get back when you sell your home if a contractor does these jobs:

PROJECT	AVERAGE COST	COST YOU WILL RECOUP
Add a Second Bathroom	$9,205	98 %
Renovate the Kitchen	17,170	95
Add a Master Bedroom and Bath	27,055	91
Add a Family Room	27,221	88
Build a Two-Story Addition	50,596	84
Remodel a Bathroom	6,443	82
Renovate the Exterior	15,450	75
Build a Deck	6,620	72

Source Remodelors Magazine

You will notice none of the improvements had a dollar-for-dollar return.

Idea 3: Raise moneywise kids.

Many parents are clueless on how to help their children make good decisions. If you do not teach them, they will make the same mistakes you made.

We learn money management from our parents. What are you teaching your kids? What are they learning by your example?

One possibility is to use allowances as teaching opportunities. An allowance will help your child learn money management, responsibility, values, goal setting, planning, and saving. These are valuable lessons in life and ones that will make your child a much happier, productive adult.

How should you give allowance?

1. Give enough—your child should be able to save money and give some charitable contributions through tithing.

2. Don't give too much—if your child can afford to buy everything he or she wants you are giving him or her too much. Your child should have to save and choose things he or she wants to buy.

3. Set a payday—setting and keeping a payday will help your child learn how to save and budget for things he or she wants to do. Keeping the payday is important; just as your budget would be thrown off if you didn't get your paycheck, so will your child's.

4. Set guidelines—if you don't want your child buying junk food, let him or her know. You may also want to set a guideline for large purchases, such as anything over thirty dollars has to be approved by you before being purchased.

5. Monitor—keeping an eye on your child's purchases will help you see when there are problems. A child who won't spend any of his or her money or a child who tries to buy friendship may need some help from you.

6. Expect mistakes—your child will have to learn how to save, and he or she may come up short sometimes, and you will have to step in with a donation. Continually bailing your child out won't help though.

7. Don't use allowance as punishment—taking money away from your child for breaking curfew won't help; however, if they break a vase, teaching them about repaying may be appropriate.

22

Biblically-based Investing—Choosing Investments That Honor Your Christian Values

Over one-third of all parables Jesus taught dealt with money. Many Christians believe the Bible tells us that everything we have is a gift from God with the potential for honoring him.

Everything we have—money, marriages, children, jobs, brains, and abilities—are gifts that we must choose to use in a way that honors him. We believe the only reason we are even created is to glorify him. As Christians, we must choose to honor God with our financial decisions.

Some Christians see that every act of spending and investing is accountable to God as an act of worship.

The key question: If you believe that every act of investing is accountable to God, should you know how your money is invested?

Today many investors use mutual funds to invest their money. The primary reason is diversification. Mutual funds allow savers to diversify their money through a number of different companies.

As a mutual fund owner, you have an undivided interest in a portfolio of stocks. The question is: do you know what stocks your mutual funds invest in?

This is also true of variable annuities that invest in sub accounts of stocks. Those sub accounts also invest in a portfolio of companies.

107

What if you own individual stocks? Are those stocks promoting the Christian values that are important to you? Do you screen your funds for companies that invest in gambling, alcohol, etc.?

The problem is that many Christians may find that their investments own specific companies whose activities and policies do not promote Christian values.

23

Advice to Newlyweds and the Role of Parents

For years I have taught a financial class at several local churches. At the heart of the class is the belief that success in marriage depends on the ability of the husband to place a priority on the emotional, spiritual, and financial well-being of the family.

Following up the class, I sit down with several couples at their request. While there are many issues in marriage, the one issue that comes up most often is money.

The heart of the issue seems to be a self-image. The biggest struggle for couples seems to be the modeling of how money should be used. In other words, what they learned from their parents and how their parents set an example in this area.

People come together in a variety of ways when getting married. Many times, parents have done a poor job of preparing their children for their financial adult life. This leads to a big part of the marital conflict couples experience.

Stewardship is a discipline. It is a learned behavior. Furthermore, if a couple has never learned the skills necessary, their marriage could be in trouble. Handling money is believed to be the number-one cause for divorce.

Here are some guidelines to consider:

1) No matter how bad your parents managed money, you can learn new ways to be a steward and honor God.

I understand bad patterns are tough to break, like alcoholism or drug abuse. Poor money management is no different. It is a tough one. The first step is to submit your marriage to God. The next step is to abide in his word. The word *abide* means to disciple or continue. It literally means to hang in there.

You must be together with your wife on this one. It requires as much seriousness as dealing with a drug addiction. As the Bible says, you can "renew" your mind. Reading this book is a good way to do it. Read other books on the subject.

2) Start tithing today; you cannot serve two masters.

Along the lines of guideline 1, good stewardship begins with tithing. Regardless of your past or present finances or your future outlook, when you trust God in this area, you transform your mind.

God promises us that when we are obedient in this area, he will reward our efforts.

3) Prepare for children.

A common mistake for young people is to live for today. Many are not concerned about savings, debt, or tithing. The common belief is that they have time and they will make more money in the future.

When you think you will have greater ability in the future to handle things, you procrastinate. Procrastinating with financial goals is a huge mistake when you understand compound interest. Remember the example about savings for college and the importance of time?

Procrastination is understandable, especially if you have heard your parents' stories about their struggles when they were first married. "We were so poor starting out; look at us now!"

What they do not tell you is that they are in debt up to their eyeballs, even at a late stage of life. Retirement is soon, and they are not ready. They do not tell you they had to cut corners in important financial areas. They are totally unprepared with no emergency savings for loss of job, disability, nursing home, or whatever else comes along. Disability and nursing home insurance is too expensive.

They've got to pay off that equity line that was used to consolidate credit cards—debt accumulated from a life of over spending. That great house they live in is financed on an interest-only ARM.

Young people seem to be really influenced by appearances. Boy, he drives a new car; he must be doing well.

Young people are ill prepared for life's surprises.

While generally it is true that you will get a promotion in the future, the missing factor is kids. Children are an endless sucking pit of money. There is always something they need: new shoes, medicine, and school.

As a parent, the greatest stress in my life is providing for the needs of my children. Regardless of whether you have the money or not, you *will* provide for the needs of your kids. There is nothing worse in life than to have your kids in need and being unable to provide for them without putting it on a credit card. This is how debt happens.

And nothing strains a marriage like debt!

The encouragement is: now is the time to prepare your finances. It is a huge mistake to think that you can wait to deal with this when you make more money. What happens is that when you make more, you spend more, especially on the kids.

God bless you!

978-0-595-42181-7
0-595-42181-4

www.ingramcontent.com/pod-product-compliance
Lightning Source LLC
Chambersburg PA
CBHW030839180526
45163CB00004B/1387